JUST AN OLD
HIPPIE

GARRY HUFF

CITI OF
BOOKS

CITIOFBOOKS, INC.
3736 Eubank NE Suite A1
Albuquerque, NM 87111-3579
www.citiofbooks.com
 Hotline: 1 (877) 389-2759
 Fax: 1 (505) 930-7244

Ordering Information:
Quantity sales. Special discounts are available on quantity purchases by corporations, associations, and others. For details, contact the publisher at the address above.

Printed in the United States of America.
ISBN-13:   Paperback   979-8-89391-630-0
                      eBook   979-8-89391-631-7

Library of Congress Control Number: 2025906998

"TAKE YOUR FUCKING HANDS OFF HER!! YOU DAMN DRUNK!!" I said as I entered through the screen door.

"Just what the hell do you think you're going to do about it little boy, if I don't?" he asked me with that drunken grin on his face.

Fear held me back until I heard my Ma scream as he slapped her to the floor. At that point, rage and anger took over and blocked out the fear. He was coming toward me with this look that told me he was going to enjoy kicking my ass.

"RUN JACK! RUN!" Ma said as she put both arms around Pa's legs trapping him. "YOU STUPID BITCH!" he said as he slapped her off his legs.

I was putting everything I had into what punches I was throwing but it was doing no good at stopping him. The last thing I remember before the blinding flash of white light was his big fist coming toward my head.

I landed on my back scooting across the hardwood floor like it was a frozen pond. My right eye was so swollen that I didn't notice the blood running down my face from the cut above my eye. With the one that I could see out of I could tell that I had knocked over the coffee table. As I slid across the floor there was a Buddha ashtray laying on the floor beside me. My mom had always told me if I was ever in trouble for me to just reach out and seek God's help. The Buddha was the only God I seen in reaching distance so I grabbed him by the head. When my Pa was close enough I kicked him in the balls and as he fell to his knees I hit him in the head with the Buddha. I did something right then that my Ma had tried for years. I introduced him to God.

I thought that it might slow him down but I never thought that it would kill him stone dead. Jack Benson senior hit the floor with the thump. His legs jerked a couple times and then he lay motionless. The gash in his head was so deep you could see the white bone of his skull. I was in a mass of confusion as I noticed the damage the Buddha had done to his head. I was glad that I had stopped him but at the same time sorry I had killed him to do it.

"OH GOD! IS HE DEAD?! Ma asked as she knelt on the floor beside us.

"I don't know." I said while thinking he was.

"You must leave here, Jack, or they will put you in jail!" Ma said trying to help me off the floor.

"It was an accident, Ma, you know that I didn't mean to kill him."

"The law isn't all you got to worry about. Your uncle Jake will kill you, if you don't leave. If you thought that Pa was a mean bastard it was Jake that had taught him everything he knew."

I hadn't thought about what Uncle Jake would do. Even if the law didn't do anything to me Uncle Jake wouldn't be so kind. "You give me the ashtray and I'll say that it was me that did it." Ma said. "No, Ma, I won't let you take the blame for what I've done." I said as I got to my feet. "You listen to me Jack; you are all I have left in this world and I'm not going to let you go to jail or let Uncle Jake kill you." Down deep I knew Ma was right if I didn't get the hell out of Ohio County I was a dead man.

So many thoughts were going through my head that it was making me dizzy. All the spinning thoughts came to a sudden stop as I thought of Joyce. What was I going to tell her after we had made love for the first time just a few weeks before? I had promised her if she would give in that I would stand by her for the rest of our lives. I didn't know that our lives would end in just a few weeks. She had saved herself and I was her first now I was being forced to break that promise I had made her.

She was just sixteen years old when her family moved to the farm next to ours. It was more of a ranch than a farm because her dad raised and sold Kentucky thoroughbred horses. Paul was always talking about Uncle Murphy that lived with us Benson's. The law according to Uncle Murphy was that 'if something could go wrong, it would, and at the worst possible time.' I had always thought he was just telling a story about Uncle Murphy until now. He was as real as it gets.

"Here, you'll need this more than me." Ma said handing me $20 and a feed sack to put my things in. I took the money and the sack from her and went to my dresser. I noticed Joyce's pictures sitting atop the dresser as I gathered my few clothes I could take with me. As I left the house I first thought of going over to Joyce's and explaining about what was going on but I stopped myself before fear of getting her and her family involved in this after they had been so good to me. I thought that Joyce would understand once she heard about my papa. At least I hoped she would. My mama's Last Words As I went out the door was don't you dare come back this way again jack Benson do you hear me she said with tears in her eyes? What was once a drizzling rain turned into a downpour in just a few minutes. it was late and I was soaked when I reach the main Highway going south.

I took my fingertips and touched them to my cut lip and swollen eye. Thinking that if someone did stop to pick me up that they would just drive on once they saw my face. The first few cars passed me as if I wasn't even there. I got to where I could tell from the sound of the tires on the wet blacktop just what kind of car was coming my way. If it was a small car the sound would be weak but if it was a big truck that was loaded it had more of a roar to it. When the car is past they would spray of fine mist on you. When the big trucks past you they would soak you. As I stared at the darkness my thoughts return to Joyce. The pain in my heart was almost as bad as the pain in my eye. I knew I was going to miss her smiles and her laughter. Most of all I was going to miss making love with her.

The van's headlights broke the darkness like a sharp knife. It was still too far away to tell what kind of car it was. Once the van had stopped I couldn't help but laugh from the way it looked. It was green and it had yellow flowers painted on it. The back door of the van slit open in a girls voice shouted to me." Are you just going to stand there she asked?" As I enter the van I could tell that it had been converted so a person could live in it. The girl turned out to be a very pretty woman and I would say she was about 10 years older than me. She was sitting in a recliner that set by the bed. The light was placed over the bed and the woman was in the shadow to wear the only part of her that was in the light was her feet.

"It's okay David you can drive on now he's inside." The voice was aimed at the blanket that hung between us and the driver. My name is Christen West she said sticking out her hand into the light. I saw a shocked look on her face came into view. "You poor thing you" she said as she set up enough to where she could touch my swollen face." Where are you headed?" a voice asked from behind the blanket." South." I said without hesitation. As David pulled back onto the highway the motion of the van caused me to sit down hard. I found myself in a squatting position. I thought of sitting on the bed but I was soaking wet and I didn't want to get these fine people mad at me right off the bat." My name is Jack Benson." I said as I shook her hand.

"We are headed for Nashville Tennessee. I'm going to cut a few records and then head for Hollywood. My stage name is cricket and my friends call me Cricket as well."

"I sure thank you for picking me up and getting me out of the rain." I said as I went ahead and set on the floor. "You don't have to sit on the floor." Cricket said pointing toward the bed. "I wouldn't want to make your boyfriend mad at me after he was nice enough to give me a ride.""
Boyfriend!" Cricket said with a laugh." Well I guess you could say he was my boyfriend but he is also my brother David. Out here on the road a singer doesn't have time for all that boyfriend trip the road is all you have.""
I'm soaking wet and it would make your bed wet if I sat on it."" You know you're right you should take off them wet things before getting into my bed." She said with a smile.

"I'm sure my other clothes are as wet as the ones I have on." I said trying to get the subject off me taking my clothes off. I smell the smoke before it appeared in the light. It was coming from the front of the van where David was driving. It was Cricket who changed the subject when she smelled the smoke.

"Pass that joint back this way." Cricket said through the curtain. As if magic a hand appeared through a hole in the blanket holding a half-smoked joint." Even if our new friend here don't smoke you know I do." Cricket joint." Even if our new friend here don't smoke you know I do." Cricket went on to say. I took the joint from the hand and passed it on to Cricket." Don't you smoke?" She asked as she took the joint for me.

"I've smoked grass before but it has been a while."

"That's a shame. "Cricket said as she blew the smoke from her hit in my face." I hate getting a buzz alone." She said handing me the joint. The smell of the pot was like a bunch of cedar. I put the joint to my lips and as I did I felt my face wrench as I touch my cut lip.

"Oh you poor thing I had Plum forgotten all about your cut lip. Here let me help you." Cricket said as she took the joint back from me. Cricket put the end of the joint in her mouth that had the fire and getting close to my face blew the smoke in my face which caused me to start coughing. Cricket took the joint from her mouth and smiled. "You have never done this before have you?" Cricket asked.

"No" was all I had to say. "All you have to do is when I blow the smoke out the end you suck it in." Cricket said as she returned the joint to her mouth. The smoke came out in a steady stream and I sucked it deep in my lungs.

The coughing took full control of my body. At first all I could see was my hand waving in front of my face. My eyes quickly blurred from the tears in them but not before seeing Cricket falling back laughing. Once Cricket got her laughter under control she apologized.

"Here try to take a drink of beer." she said handing me a cold opened beer. I put the beer to my lips and drink and as soon as I took the can for my mouth Cricket started blowing smoke in my face again. I was surprised that it really worked I didn't cough that time. We both felt the van jerk to one side and start to slow down to a complete stop. The movement of the van caused our lips to come together. Our lips came together with such force that it had to hurt but I was so stoned by then that I didn't feel it.

"Piss break." David said as he came through the blanket curtain.

David stuck his head through the whole first and the way the blanket lay over his shoulders made him look like a deer head on the wall. "Well sis you sure are wasting time after what pop always said that time was too short and life to waste any of it."

"I wouldn't want Jack here to think I was too easy." Cricket said with a laugh. "And besides he already thinks you're a jealous boyfriend instead of being my little brother."

"You don't have to worry about me Jack only have love for Cricket as a brother. From the looks of your eye you already run into enough jealous boyfriends for one night."

"I was mugged by a few boys back in a small town before you picked me up. "It was a lot and I knew it but I had to get them off the subject as soon as possible.

Then David went to the cooler and pulled out another cold beer and handed it to me as Cricket opened the van door and stepped out into the rain. "What did you do with the joint Cricket?"

David asks as if Cricket was still with us. "I think she put it in the ashtray." David reached down and pulled what was left of the joint from the ashtray. There's nothing left he said as he examined the roach.

"You boys had better hurry up and make it quick because it really is starting to pour down out there.

"Hey sis did you know I just got one hit off that last joint?"

"Well you will just have to roll us another one." She said as she came back in.

"Hand me that can over there." David said pointing toward a Prince Albert can.

"Sure" I said and handed him the can. He opened the can and pulled out the rolling papers.

He folded the paper with one hand and poured the pot from the can right into the paper as he brought the paper to his mouth to lick it. Just by using his fingers on one hand he just rolled his thumb and it came out a rolled joint. David put the joint in the ashtray and told Cricket not to light it until we got back.

I followed him out into the darkness and the cold rain. It didn't take long for the cold rain to chill me to the bone. I know it was cold because as I stood pissing I could see the hot steam come off the piss as it hit the ground. I finished before David and hurried back to the van door that was still open. Cricket was standing beside the bed and nothing but her pants. She picked up a housecoat and slipped it on. She had a very beautiful body for a woman of her age I thought firm very firm.

"I had hoped that I would be dressed by the time you two got back." Cricket said apologetically. "You have a lovely body, to hide it would be a sin."

"I don't think a person has the right to complain about their bodies. If it's good enough for the maker then we have no right to be ashamed of our bodies. I'm not ashamed of my body." Cricket said as she open the housecoat. "Damn sis, I've heard of fast women but you take the cake." Dave said as he came back in. "It's not what you think little brother. I was just showing Jack that I wasn't ashamed of my body."

"That's one thing about my sister she likes to show off her body to as many people as possible." "Close the door before I bend you over my knee like I used to do." As soon as we got back underway David asked me to pass him his beer and Joint in the ashtray. I did.

I must have had a worried look on my face because Cricket assured me he could handle it. I think she said that to try to convince herself more than me.

"You poor thing get those wet clothes off, you look like you're drowning."

"I don't think that it would do any good to put on my other pants because they are as wet as the ones I have on." Cricket stood up and took off her house coat and handed it to me. I stared in amazement as she stood there in just her panties.

"You wear this and I'll put on a t-shirt if that will make you a tease." Cricket said as she handed me the house coat. As soon as I took it from her she went to the foot of the bed and picked out a long t-shirt and used it for a night shirt. Cricket unzip the sleeping bag that lay on top of the bed and climbed in. I could feel her eyes on me as I started undressing.

It's time you practice what you preach I heard her say without saying a word. After telling Cricket that she should not be ashamed of her body now I was in the spotlight. Once I got my shirt and shoes off my pants more or less rolled off. I don't know if it was the cool night air or the fact that a woman was watching me but one or the other was giving me cold chills. Goosebumps covered both my arms and legs." You chicken. You after all that talk about not being ashamed of our bodies "Cricket said with a laugh. "I knew you were just talk. "Once I got my pants off I just stood there in my underwear.

"It's for your own good." I said over my shoulder keeping my back to her.

"How will I know what is good for me if I can't see it?" That struck me as funny and I started laughing. It cause my cut lip to hurt but I couldn't stop myself.

"Your underwear to." Cricket said "You can't get in this warm bed with wet underwear on." I started to say that she got to keep hers on when hers hit me in the chest and fell to my feet. I know that I'm 17 but I didn't need a written letter to tell me what Cricket had on her mind. Thank God that my life was granted to me in the free loving generation. I didn't bother to put on the house coat I just pulled off my underwear and climbed in the bed with Cricket the sleeping bag was designed for one person so the only way we can both fit is to lie front to back or one on top of the other. I didn't know Cricket well enough to start off on top of her. Cricket scooted as far back as she could to let me in. Cricket molded her body to me in the warmth of her took the chill away.

Hot blood started rushing through my veins as I laid down. Cricket reached above her head and turned off the light. After she molded herself back in place I got to thinking what is wrong with this picture everything seems to be working right but there is something not right. That's what I realize that the pretty naked woman was behind me. As I turned my shoulder to make me turn Cricket moved her hand to stop me." We are not going to have sex tonight. "She whispered in my ear.

"We're not." I asked in a completely confused state. "No not in the same way you are thinking. I just want to feel your body against mine." Started to tell her that I wasn't into playing games when I felt Cricket's hot hand on my penis stopped me in my tracks. The one thing that Joyce taught me was that there was a thousand ways to have sex without having sex.

I close my eyes and pretended it was Joyce back there." No, no." she whispered as I tried to roll onto my back. Cricket released my throbbing penis long enough to pull my left arm behind me and placed it between her legs. Cricket placed her left knee on my left hip. A first felt how course her pubic hair was it felt like a very fine hair brush. The lower I took my fingers the wetter they became. My Sensitive fingertips eagerly searched for the tiny bud that always drove Joyce wild. I could tell when I found it by the way Cricket stopped her hand and squeeze my penis. I lowered my fingers until they reached her wetted entrance. I took my middle finger and parted her lips and dipped my finger. I dipped my finger in her wetness then brought the moisture to her clit. As my finger touched crickets clit a gasp escaped her lip.

Cricket increase the up-and-down motion as I returned my fingers to the well for another taste of honey. As I started my fingers tour cricket split for the second time she placed her hand on mine to stop me.

The way her fingers lay on top of mine she got in my fingers to her entrance and shoved it.

Her mouth was right at my ear when I heard a moan escape her lips. Her walls encircled my finger like a moist glove. My thumb parted the lips of her clit and searched for her bud again. After just a few strokes cricket was wet enough for me to add another finger. With each stroke of my two fingers cricket was matching me with strokes.

"Make love to me Joyce!" I yelled before I thought. The words had no more gotten out of my mouth when I realized what I had done.

I was hoping that Cricket had not heard my mistake but when I opened my eyes I knew she had heard every word. I could see flames of anger in her eyes even in the dark. Cricket held her temper but she let me know that the sex was over with.

"I'm sorry Cricket." I said as she climbed over me getting out of bed. Cricket was at the foot of the

bed putting on a pair of bell bottoms as I swing my legs over the side of the bed and sat up. I was trying to think of a better way to apologize when she went to the chair and sat down.

The overhead light only shines in the one direction in the only part of cricket that I could see in the light was her feet.

"That shit happens" she finally said. I couldn't see her face but I could tell by the way her voice broke that she was crying.

The silence was only broken by the sound of a beer being opened.

Damn what was her problem anyway she thought to herself the guy tried to apologize didn't he. He must love her very much. That was what hurt cricket so much. She had no one who loved her like that. "Does she love you as much as you do her?", she asked.

"Yes, I think so." was the only answer I could give.

"I'm sorry I hurt your feelings." I said "that was not my intention."

"I'm not mad at you as I am me" she said.

"I'm a grown woman and I've been acting like a little school girl. "I reached and picked up the house coat from where I had dropped it in the floor and put it on.

Cricket set and rolled a joint and then handed me a beer. "If you take a drink of beer before you take a hit you won't cough so much."

Cricket's hand appeared out of the darkness holding a lit joint.

I took it from her.

I did as she said and to my surprise it worked.

Cricket took another long draw off the joint and the light off it showed the outline of her face.

David pulled the van off the highway into a rest stop and shut off the motor.

"I'm too tired to go any longer." David said as he came through the curtain. "Come on sis move to the bed. You know I sleep in the chair."

Cricket handed David the joint as she raised from the chair and come to the bed.

You sleep in the back side she said as she climbed in bed. This time she was laying in front of me. If there is going to be any hanky panky sis just keep it quiet. "There isn't going to be any hanky-panky little brother that I promise you."

I think she said that for my benefit more than David's.

We laid in silence for a while and the last thing I remember saying was I'm sorry.

Cricket woke early the next morning when Jack started moaning and jerking as if someone was beating the shit out of him. At first she thought Jack was trying to have sex with her. Jumping from the bed she was a few feet from it before turning around. Was Jack pretending to be asleep or what is he having a bad dream? It was hard to tell with his eyes swollen shut.

"What's wrong sis?" David asked from the chair." Oh nothing Jack is just having a bad dream I think."

My hair was stuck to my forehead because I was sweating so bad. "Should we wake him?" David asked raising from the chair. Cricket and David both were quiet as a church mouse as they got out of the van and closed the door.

"I picked this place because it has showers and a restaurant." David said coming up behind Cricket.

"How long before we reach the farm?" Cricket asked him without turning around.

"We should be there in about 2 hours." he said." Do you think we should ask Jack to come along with us." Cricket asked. "Well they did say it was for anyone who believed in Brotherly Love." David said with a little laugh. David's facial expression changed as he asked Cricket if Jack had done anything to her that he should know about.

"No little brother there's nothing you need to know about." David knew that he wasn't going to get any more information from Cricket but he also knew if she had been hurt she would have told him. I must have woke up when David closed the van door! I remember opening my one good eye and the other being swelled shut. When I noticed that Cricket and David were both gone I thought that I must have lost my ride last night from my fuck up. Cricket was probably telling David to get rid of me right now. I thought as I put on my wet clothes. They were both looking at me as I came out of the van packing my bag of clothes and wearing my wet clothes.

"Are you leaving us?" Cricket asked as she came walking up to me.

"I thought after last night you might want me to."

"All I want you to do is quit apologizing." Cricket said.

"Have you been to a commune ?" David asked as he reached us.

"A what?" I ask not knowing what he was saying.

"A commune." Cricket said trying to find the best way to make me understand.

"A place where a bunch of people camp out together."

"I've heard of them but I never been to one."

"Well that's where we're headed and your welcome to come with us." She finally said.

"That's the best offer I've had all day." I said putting my things back in the van. After putting on the dry clothes that David lent me we were on the road again. David started telling me all he had been told about where we were going.

"It's a big plantation that sold slaves before the war between the states. It's got lots of one room houses on it and every body has to work. There are lots of single girls there that sleep with different men every night." David said to me with a wink.

"Don't you know that Tom just told you that to get you to come down here." Cricket quickly said with a frown that told David she had seen the wink.

"You must be some kind of dumb ass to believe that every women in the place has the hots for you."

I may have been a few years younger than David but I didn't buy that story either.

"Well what did Kim tell you about it?" David asked.

"Kim is a girl, I mean woman, who was my roommate in collage. And Kim told me, "Cricket said with a laugh at the end pointed a finger at her little brother. "She said that just a few people had houses and that you have to know the right people to get one."

"I wouldn't want to keep you from getting a house." I said to cricket.

"I don't think that will be a problem." She said to me with a smile on her face.

"Well Jack who do you believe?" David asked.

"All we can do is hope, isn't it David?" I ask grinning from ear to ear. We reached the commune about nine o'clock in the morning and the fields were full of people. The rolls of corn seemed to go on forever. It may have been cold and wet the night before but the sun now was hot even at nine o'clock in the morning. As we got closer to the buildings I could see that some if the people had made sleeping rooms out of what they could get their hands on. The long houses David had been talking about turned out to be slave quarters. Most were in worst shape then the barn that set close to the buildings. We were directed to Tom's office by a man who seemed to be lost himself.

"I'd say he was stoned out if his mind." David said as we all got out of the van.

"I've been stoned a lot in my life and I would have to agree." Cricket said.

Tom Harder sat at his desk looking over some papers when the three of us entered his office. He knew David and Cricket but he didn't know the young man with the busted up face.

"David and Cricket, how glad I am to see that you made it." Tom said as he came around the desk.

"Tom this is a friend of ours. This is Jack Benson. We thought it would be alright if he could stay with us." Cricket said. "Are you in trouble with the law?" Tom asked

"No!" I said hoping he couldn't tell I was lying.

"It's okay with me but I could only get two cabins, so he'll have to stay with either you or David."

"Well he's not staying in my cabin." David blurted out.

"He won't have to stay in either of our cabins." Cricket said. She had all of our attention.

"Okay where is he staying if it's not with you or David?" Tom asked just as lost as me and David.

"He can stay in the van after David and me get our things out."

"That will be fine with me if its ok with Jack." All three heads turn to me.

"It's better then a cardboard box out in the field." I said with a smile.

Kim came through the door and threw her arms around her ex collage room mate. "Cricket girl you are as pretty as you was back at collage."

"That's just your bed side manner talking." Cricket said with a laugh. Kim turned her attention to me. Walking over and placing her hand over my swollen eye. "Your running a temp." Her fingers did feel cool to my face.

"Jack this is my best friend Kim, and she is the closest thing to a doctor in this camp."

Kim grabbed my arm and lead me to the door. "Jack if you'll follow me I'll show you where the aid station is."

Cricket didn't like the feeling she had in the pit of her stomach, pull yourself together girl, Cricket said to herself. You only known him for two days and he doesn't belong to you. Still Cricket also knew Kim and the way she went through collage in a different bed for the whole four years. As Cricket turned and looked at David she was surprised to see David looking at Jack and Kim walk away arm in arm. His eyes were locked on Kim. Do you think that him and her had done it she asked herself.

Once Kim and I reached the first aid station Kim got an ice pack from the freezer." Hold this on your eye while I get the stuff I'll need to clean your cuts."

"How long have you known David and Cricket?" I asked. "Tom and I met Cricket in college and we met David after I graduated."

"I didn't know that Cricket had gone to college." I said.

"Well she went for one year before she had to quit." I got my Nursing degree and Tom got his in chemistry." Kim said as she sat a bottle of orange stuff on the tray next to me. As I looked out the window with my good eye I couldn't help but wonder what two people with so much knowledge were doing in a place like this. "If you'll take off your shirt and lay back I'll put some drops in your eyes so it will heal faster." Kim's eyes watched every move I made as I took off my shirt as she requested. Once I got laid down I turned my head to one side so I could see what Kim was doing.

I hadn't thought that a nurse would be wearing white cotton pants but Kim was. You could see the white outline of her panties through her pants. She has a nice round ass on her I thought as she walked away from me. I'll bet she looks as good coming toward me as she does going. Tom came through the door before she turned around and by that time he had my attention to. "How is our new man doing?" He asked as he entered the room.

"Oh, he'll live." Kim said not trying to hide the sarcasm in her voice.

Tom knew that Kim was still mad at him from last night but she had never showed it in front of a patient before. Tom knew that Kim had never been so mad at him before either. It seems that Tom was out selling his drugs when he came across Shafaun. It seems Shafaun wanted drugs and didn't have any money.

Tom solved the problem by giving her the drugs for some pussy. Tom hadn't expected Kim to come looking for him let alone find him. It hadn't been the first time that he had made that deal but it was the first time he got caught.

"Mr. Benson, here is the list of rules we have here we like to call the Ten Commandments." Tom said with the little laugh. Tom handed me the list.

"Tom leave the young man alone for now. I'm sure he isn't going to break any of your rules before tomorrow," the sarcasm had returned to Kim's voice. "Besides after I put these eye drops in his eyes he will have to stay out of the sun for at least 12 hours." Kim said. Tom left without saying another word.

"You will have to stay out of the Sun for a few hours." Kim said as she put the eye drops in. Whatever it was that Kim had put in my eye it sure burned. Tears was rolling out of my eye as if I were crying. I started to bring my right hand up and rub my burning eye but Kim caught me by the wrist.

"Don't rub your eye." Kim said" It will only make things worse." Kim's long black hair came almost to her waist. It was pulled into a ponytail that made it look like a long black rope. Kim's eyes were as dark brown as to look black. Kim was holding the ice pack on my eye now and had laid my hand down close to her crotch. I found myself getting an erection and knew if I didn't move my hand it was on its way to becoming a full grade hard on. I pulled my hand back down to my side with such force that Kim realized what she had done and backed up a little.

"I'll make a patch for your so the sun won't hurt it on your way home. Be sure and stay out of the sun for at least 6 hours." Kim said again as she put the patch on my eye. It was getting close to high noon and the sun was as hot now as it would be this afternoon. Tom stood at his office door and watched as I left the first aid station.

"It sure took him long enough." He said in a whisper even though he was the only person there. "She needs me." he said to himself. "She needs me." He kept saying as his eyes moved back to Kim. Down deep Tom knew that the only reason Kim was here was because of him. She could go to any hospital and make three times the money she was getting here. If everything worked out right Kim wouldn't want for money again. He would see to that.

"I see you, you bastard!" Kim said as she watched Tom standing in his doorway. The way he was watching Jack as he walked away from the Aid Station told her that Tom was just a little jealous.

"By the time I'm through with you you bastard you will be green with the jealousy." Kim remember telling Tom back in college that there wasn't going to be any strings attached to their relationship. She had always thought that Tom was being faithful until last night when she caught him fucking that whore. She looked at Jack as he vanished from sight. He may be a few years younger but he had the hard rock body of a man. He got such a fine body from hard work that she was sure. Kim felt a tingle between her legs just thinking about Jack. She was going to have him, she told herself.

Kim was still thinking of Jack as a 10 year old girl came running through the door. She was saying something about her mother had lost her water.

"Slow down little girl and tell me what you're trying to say." Once the little girl caught her breath she told Kim that her mother was having a baby and that her water broke and she was in labor. Kim gathered up the stuff she thought she would need and left with the little girl leading the way. They arrived at a tent made of a few sheets of plastic the woman had just about delivered the baby before Kim had reached her. All Kim had to do was cut the umbilical cord and clean up the after birth. Kim felt she had been lucky so far but she wondered what she would do if it had been a breech birth.

The first place David went was to the first aid station. Finding that the place was empty he turned to leave. David thought of going over to Tom's office to see if Kim was over there but decided against it. The rain from the night before was making the heat humid, sticky, and hot. David hadn't walked very far when he felt his shirt and it was soaked. He had sweated so much that it looked like someone had thrown a bucket of water on him. The only shade David saw was a large tree at the end of a row of cabins. David sat down to where he could lean up against the trunk of the tree. He noticed that the field in front of him was a big garden. It seemed to go on forever. This is where the people grew their food. The people working the garden looked like different colored dots in a sea of green.

"Are you alright?" A voice asked from behind him. David turned to see who had asked him the question she was Shafaun Copper. Her father was a light-skinned black man and her mother was a South Vietnam. She lived in Nashville up until her mother died a few months back. Her father had been in the Army and after he had moved her he had gotten killed. She was hated so much by the homes in the neighborhood that after her mother died she had to leave. Shafaun was pleasing to the eyes to say the least.

Her long black hair layed across her back like a black cape. Her breast looked to be as solid as a cantaloupe. She had her father's eyes with the way they seemed to reach forever.

"Yes I'm alright just a little hot."

"Would you like a glass of water?" She asked.

"I'm just a little thirsty." David said looking up at the girl without saying another word. The girl left him setting and went into the end apartment of the building. In just a few minutes she returned carrying a tall glass of water." You haven't been here very long have you?" she asked as she handed me the glass. "No. I just got here." David said as he took the glass." Is it that easy to tell?" David asked.

"It sure enough is white boy! This here is where they put their nigers on this old plantation.

"I'm not prejudice David said trying to convince Shafaun that he wasn't like that.

"Do you know how many eyes are honest at this very minute?"

"No." David replied.

"Enough that you should drink up and get out before the wrong ones find you here."

"I've done nothing to anyone black or white!" David said in a loud voice.

"Look here white boy! Just because you claim not to be prejudiced does not mean that no one is so drink the water and get the hell out for your own good!" Shafaun said.

"My name is David." David said getting in a stand.

"What is your name?" He asked handing Shafaun back the glass.

"There is no need for you to know my name. I'm sure we won't meet again." Shafaun said taking the glass from David.

"Have it your way." David said as he turned and walked back the way he came.

Except for a few kids playing in front of their living quarters David saw no one.

As he walked out he could feel the eyes watching his every move.

Tom was on the phone as David entered his office." I've been down to the gardens and watch the people working." David said not waiting for Tom to hang up.

"I don't think that I want to work out there in the fields."

David said" Well, that's okay David! I didn't bring you down here to work in the fields. I hadn't planned to tell you this until later but now is a good time as any." Tom said.

"What is it that you did bring me down here for?" David asked.

"David there is over a thousand people living here at any given time. All those people that got one thing in common they like to get high. I plan to supply all those people with what they want. I'm willing to pay you $500 a week to grow mushrooms for me."

As soon as David heard how much money Tom was going to pay he just knew that it wouldn't be legal. "Why me ?" David asked.

"It's simple. You know how to grow things." Tom said.

"How many laws do I have to break to get five hundred dollars a week?" David asked.

"That's what I've been trying to tell you. You can hire another man to help you grow mushrooms. Growing mushrooms is not illegal. Do you trust that boy with you?"

"You mean Jack?" David asked.

"Yes, that's him. Do you trust him?" Tom replied.

"I've only known him for two days but yeah I trust him." David exclaimed. Tom studied David before he told him to go ahead and tell him he can work with you.

"Are you going to pay him the same?"

"No not at first, but it will depend on what he does. You better not tell anyone what I'm paying you. We'll just keep that between us." Tom said.

"Have it your way." David said as he left the office.

Kim knew that Tom was fucking around on her and after last night she wondered for how long? How often had he tried to get her to marry him? She knew that it had been her that had refused to make a vow to sleep with

Except for a few kids playing in front of their living quarters David saw no one.

As he walked out he could feel the eyes watching his every move.

Tom was on the phone as David entered his office." I've been down to the gardens and watch the people working." David said not waiting for Tom to hang up.

"I don't think that I want to work out there in the fields."

David said" Well, that's okay David! I didn't bring you down here to work in the fields. I hadn't planned to tell you this until later but now is a good time as any." Tom said.

"What is it that you did bring me down here for?" David asked.

"David there is over a thousand people living here at any given time. All those people that got one thing in common they like to get high. I plan to supply all those people with what they want. I'm willing to pay you $500 a week to grow mushrooms for me."

As soon as David heard how much money Tom was going to pay he just knew that it wouldn't be legal. "Why me ?" David asked.

"It's simple. You know how to grow things." Tom said.

"How many laws do I have to break to get five hundred dollars a week?" David asked.

"That's what I've been trying to tell you. You can hire another man to help you grow mushrooms. Growing mushrooms is not illegal. Do you trust that boy with you?"

"You mean Jack?" David asked.

"Yes, that's him. Do you trust him?" Tom replied.

"I've only known him for two days but yeah I trust him." David exclaimed. Tom studied David before he told him to go ahead and tell him he can work with you.

"Are you going to pay him the same?"

"No not at first, but it will depend on what he does. You better not tell anyone what I'm paying you. We'll just keep that between us." Tom said.

"Have it your way." David said as he left the office.

Kim knew that Tom was fucking around on her and after last night she wondered for how long? How often had he tried to get her to marry him? She knew that it had been her that had refused to make a vow to sleep with only each other. "Damn!" She exclaimed as she stomped her foot on the wooden floor. Kim started to entertain the idea of using David to make Tom jealous but decided that Jake would work better at making him jealous. If for no other reason was his young age I wonder if he if he is fucking Cricket or maybe he's a cherry? That would be to much to hope for. Kim thought. Looking out the window just in time to see Jack and Cricket heading towards the public showers. That was one thing she hadn't thought about, Cricket is her best friend. If Cricket had something going with Jack then she would leave him alone, but if she doesn't hes fair game.

Just as Jack and Cricket left her sight Tom stepped up on her porch.

"What do you want now?" Kim asked as Tom came through the door.

"I was wanting to talk to you Kim, about last night." Tom said as he hopped up on the table.

"There is nothing you can say to me Tom to make me trust you again"

"Last night was the first time I did anything like that. I promise you, Kim. You are the only one for me."

"And I'm suppose to just take your word for it and forget what I saw?!" Kim exclaimed.

"No I'm not asking you to forget. I'm asking you to forgive me?"

"Tom I know that was the one to say that we could be with other people. But until last night I never had to face my words. I'm just need some time to think this over." Kim stated then left.

Tom and Kim's cabin was one of the few that had running water.

Kim had picked up a sack of clothes as she left. Heading straight for the public showers. The water from the showers comes straight from the lake outside. It didn't go through a water heater so it was cool as it came out of the shower heads.

After the first cool shock of the water felt good on Crickets body. She was letting the spray hit her in the face so her eyes where closed when Kim came up behind her. Kim tapped Cricket on the shoulder.

"Don't use up the whole lake." Kim said with a laugh.

"Ha sister I been thinking about you all day." Cricket said.

"Apparently I'm not the only one thing on your mind." Kim said pointing to a hickey on Crickets neck.

Cricket blushed as she told Kim that it was Jacks way of thanking her for a ride. That's all.

"Makes me want to run out and buy a car just to pick up hitch hikers." Kim said with a laugh. Kim could have told Cricket that she came down here to find out more about her and Jack. Yet with one look at that hickey on Crickets neck answered all her questions.

"How are things with you and Tom?"

"Oh just fine." Kim said forcing a smile.

"We'll have to get together soon." Cricket said as she stepped out of the shower.

"I was just going to say that." Kim replied. "Why don't you and David and Jake come for supper Kim asked as she followed Cricket out to the dressing room.

"I'll ask the ask the boys but I'm sure they will be in for it."

"I'll just tell Tom to through a few more burgers on the grill."

"Do you think that David would feel out of place?'" Cricket asked.

As I came out of the showers, I didn't see Cricket anywhere.

"She must have had some urgent business." Kim said as she came up behind me. At first I didn't know who she was out of uniform.

"Hows the eye?" She asked as she reached up and touched the wet patch. "This will not do." Kim said as she pulled the wet patch off. "Follow me to the first aid station and I'll put a new one on." I was surprised to find out that the swelling had gone down enough that I could see out of it.

"Thanks anyway but I don't think I will need another one." I said as I walked off. If Kim wasn't Crickets best friend, I would have taken her up on the offer of a second trip to the first aid station. I thought as Kim fell in behind me as I walked. My old man had always said that it was a crazy man that tried to hole two gardens at once. Now I know what he was talking about.

David went to the van first. Not finding Jack there, he went to Crickets cabin. The door was unlocked so he just walked in. Finding no one there either he turned to leave.

"I'm glad your here." Cricket said as she came up behind him.

"Oh, there you are sis have I got news for you."

"Well I've got some good news too." Cricket said as she sat down on the bed and started rolling a joint.

"I talked to Tom and he is going to give me and Jack a job that pays five hundred a week." David said as he sat down beside her.

"Little brother this is 1969 and I know that two people don't make five hundred a week for hoeing a garden."

"He wants me and Jack to grow mushrooms for him." David replied.

"Well I'm going to ask him all about it tonight when we go over there."

Cricket said.

"You what?" Tom asked when Kim told him about inviting the three of us over for a BBQ. Tom had been with Kim long enough that he knew it would do no good to try to change her mind. "I'll need to go to the liqour store and get some more to drink."

"You will need to find David a woman to keep him company." Kim said as Tom started to leave.

"Why should I find David a woman, fuck him, he can find his own woman!"

"Now Tom, you know that it was you that insisted that David come down here. We know from last night that you know plenty of woman. Don't we?" Kim asked with a frown. Tom remembered how long it took him to convince her to move to the commune and how little it would take to make her leave.

Shafaun Blake was a woman who was of two back grounds. Her father was a black US Army Sargent and her mother was a Vietnam bar girl. The blend gave her a light brown skin. Her eyes was as black as her long hair. Her and her mother lived on the post housing until her father was killed in action in Vietnam. Her mother couldn't take all the resentment that she had to endour on a regular basis so she went back to Vietnam. Shafaun was twenty years old when her father died so she stayed here in the US. She had been on the road for the last two years. Shafaun didn't exactly know when she got hooked on drugs. It just seemed that she woke up one morning and she couldn't do without them.

The black man that had brought her here had kept her in drugs but in return she had to have sex with whom ever he wanted her to. That's how she had meet Tom in the first place. Her so called boyfriend had made a deal with Tom. If Tom would give him fifty hits of acid he could fuck his girl. It seems Tom paid him up front and while Shafaun and Tom were fucking he took of with everything she had. She was lucky that Tom was in charge of housing so he let her stay in the cabin. Tom would bring her food at least once a week and sometimes twice a week. Each time he would take it out in trade. It wasn't that she didn't get anything from Tom either. Tom was good looking for a white man.

Tom had placed Shafaun in the black section of the commune on purpose. Kim wouldn't think to look fir him there or so he thought till last night. Shafaun had known about Kim from the start but didn't dare go around her. That was Toms first rule. When Shafaun saw Tom pull up in his car in broad daylight it was some what of a shock. Was he here to run her off or buy some pussy, she asked herself.

"This is quiet a surpprise." Shafaun said as Tom came through the door. Still not sure what he there for Shafaun took off her shirt and tossed it to the floor. She decided to wait until he spoke before taking off her shorts.

"I'm not here for that Shafaun. I'm here on a mission for Kim."

"I understand." Shafaun said as she got up to gather her few things.

"Kim and I are having a cook out and we want you to be a date for a guest."

"You have to be the dumbest white boy I've ever seen." Shafaun said with a laugh. "Your lady friend caught us fucking last night and now your telling me she wants to have me over for supper."

"There's going to be other people there, that's what you are needed for." Tom said in an angry voice. "You will be a date for a friend of mine and if your are good to him, there will be more." Tom knew that this could blow up in his face but he was tired of playing Kim's games. She will either come around or she will leave and at the moment he didn't give a damn which. Tom went out letting the screen door slam behind him. For what he planned for David, he was going to be his best friend. He found himself with a little smile on his face because he knew that once David had sex with Shafaun he would be hooked too.

Kim had told me about the BBQ before we parted. She had said that it was Crickets idea and I had believed her. Cricket was rolling a joint as I walked in. Once she was finished she handed me the pot and papers telling me to put them in my pocket.

"We were invited to a BBQ over Toms and Kims!" Cricket said as she lit the joint'. "Did Tom say anything to you about you and David working for him for five hundred dollars a week?" Cricket asked as she passed me the joint.

"No, he never said a thing to me." I replied as I took the joint from her. "I haven't talked to Tom or David since this morning." I give Cricket the 'no thank you' jester as she tried to hand the joint back to me.

"Here I'll take that." David said as he entered the room. "I knew you two were getting high when I heard all that coughing."

"Did Tom say anything to you about me working with you?" I ask. Davids lungs was full of smoke to where he couldn't talk but he was able to shake his head yes. Once he was able to talk again David started telling me what Tom had told him.

"Yes, he wanted me to ask you if you wanted to work with me. So that's what I'm doing."

"How much is he going to pay and what is the job?" Jack asked.

"You said that he was paying you five hundred a week." Cricket said still not believing, that David must have gotten the figures wrong she thought.

"He offered me that. He didn't say what he was going to pay Jack."

"We'll straighten that out when we get there." Cricket said as she went out the door. David put what was left of the joint in the ashtray and followed Cricket out the door.

Tom wasn't there when we got there. Kim and Cricket sat on the small couch and David and I sat on the table. Kim picked up a half smoked joint and lit it. Cricket was high already but took the joint anyway. She tried to pass the joint to me but I told her to go ahead because I had enough.

"Suit yourself!" She said as she passed it back to Kim.

Tom came through the door caring two cases of beer."Looks like you all got a head start on me!" Tom said without cracking a smile.

"Just a little one." Kim said with a laugh.

"Who wants a beer?" Tom asked as he was putting away the beer. The pot had given us all the dry mouth so we all took one.

"Who's at the door?" Kim asked as she raised from the couch to answer the door."May I help you?" Kim asked thinking the beautiful black girl was there for some medical reason.

"I'm Shafaun the blind date for your guest. Tom asked me to come here." Shafaun said looking at the woman that was stoned out of her head.

"I told him a blind date not a black date." Kim said with a laugh.

Kim turned to Tom and her smile left her face."Since you invited her, why don't you introduce your friend Tom!"

"Yes I'll do that!" Tom said as Kim and Shafaun entered the room. "This is my lady friend Kim. This young lady over here is her good friend from collage, Cricket." Turning to me and David he said "This will be your date David. David is Crickets brother and this young man with the war wounds is Mr. Jack Benson."

Shafaun was relieved to learn that she didn't have a date with the young man with the wounds. "HA! I know you." David said rising from the table to greet Shafaun. Even Tom was surprised that David had met Shafaun already. "This young lady gave me water when I was thirsty!" David said to explain every bodies surprise. The way Shafaun talked and laughed like old friends, Kim decided to give Tom a shadow of doubt and accept Shafaun as a date for David.

She knew that Tom could be a good man when he wanted to be. If this had been the woman he had been seeing then the only thing she could say about Tom was that, he sure had good taste. Her bronze skin was outlined by her long black hair. Kim could swear that her eyes were as black as her hair. The tight fitting halter top showed two firm breasts straining to get out from beneith the material. Her bell bottoms showed a big round ass trying the same thing the breast were.

Cricket was watching Kim look at Shafaun with hunger in her eyes. She wondered if Kim had gone back to the way she was in collage? How many times had she looked at her like that when they were room mates. Cricket had put off her advances for six months before she gave in.

"Is it because your stoned or is it something else?" Jack asked. Cricket realized she was starring at Shafaun too. Jacks question brought Cricket out of a self imposed trance.

Tom shook Shafauns hand like he was meeting her for the first time."You play your cards right and I'll make it worth your while." He said in a whisper. Shafaun knew she had Tom over a barrel and she was going to get as much as she could out of him and his drug dealings. Shafaun went to the couch and sat down next to Cricket and Kim.

"How did you come by a name of a bug that rubs its legs together and makes a noise?" Shafasun asked.

"It's a stage name and what a crickett does when it rubs its legs together is make music for another crickett." Cricket said.

"I had never thought of it like that before." Shafaun said.

"I would say it's time to fire up the grill and start this BBQ started." Tom said as he headed for the door. I first thought of sitting and talking to the girls until Kim asked me where I was from. I decided that it was time for me to get the fuck out of there. "A small town in Kentucky!" I said as I went out the door.

"David you should go help Jack and Tom while we have a little girl talk." Kim said. After David left the girls sat in silence for a few minutes. Shafaun broke the silence by asking Cricket what kind of music she played.

"Did you see how Kim was looking at Shafaun?" David asked as he approached us.

"what are you trying to say?" Tom asked angrily.

"I'm not trying to say anything." David said after he realized that he was talking without thinking again. Tom couldn't get mad at David for what he had said because he had noticed it to.

I got both of their attention when I said that Shafaun had gotten all of our attention. Tom got his anger under control once he thought of how right I was.

Shafaun felt the first twinge of fear when Kim asked where she met Tom. She quickly recovered and told her that her ex boyfriend had brought her here but had run off and left her here. Tom had been kind enough to let her stay on by herself. Shafaun felt a little relieved as she watched to see if Kim thought she was telling the truth. She did so Shafaun breathed a sigh of relief.

The three girls sat and smoked the biggest part of a joint. "Why don't we take the rest of this out to the boys." Kim said as she rose and headed for the door.

"I guess if we want anymore of that joint we had better go with her." Cricket said.

"I guess your right!" Shafaun said rising from the couch and followed

Kim out the door. Cricket followed her out because she was curious about what Jack was doing, not because she wanted more of the joint.

Shafaun was more interested in getting LSD off Tom but didn't want to just ask in front of the other girls. She could tell from the way that the other two girls talked that they knew nothing of the deal Tom made with her. She decided to keep her mouth shut until the right time.

While we were standing around the BBQ David asked Tom to tell us more about the work me and him were going to be doing for the job.

"Well you two will be growing mushrooms and he would be taking them and making acid out off them." The word acid brought a frown to my face because I was thinking battery acid. I didn't know battery acid was made out of mushrooms.

"Look out there !" Tom said pointing to all the people out in the commune. "There is at least five hundred people out there every day looking for a way of getting a buzz." Tom replied.

"I hate to burst your bubble Tom but I don't know the first thing about turning mushrooms into acid."

"Don't you think I know that!" Tom said angrily. "I will be the one who will do what it takes to turn the mushrooms into acid!" Tom said angrily. "Now don't say anything to Kim." Tom replied calmer. "I just don't think she will understand."

"I don't think Cricket would go for that either." David said."She don't like me selling pot let alone acid." They both were looking at me to see if I was going to go along with them.

"Well I wouldn't want Shafaun to know." I said with a laugh.

"What are you laughing at?" Kim asked as she came up to where we were standing."That sure smells good !" Cricket said as she came up to where I was standing. Shafaun stood beside David and that left Kim and Tom facing each other.

"Oh well!" Kim said as she brought a smile to her face. A warmth came over Tom as he saw the smile appear. Everyone's attention went to David as he finished off his beer and let out a very loud belch.

"Your the first one to finish doing so why don't you go get us another round." Tom said as he started taking the meat off the grill.

"Sure I can do that." David said as he started for the house. "I'll help!" Shafaun offered.

"Just imagine that." Kim said."How long has it been since it took two people to carry a six pack?" Tom couldn't help but laugh when he heard Kim say something like that. Turning to me Kim walked up to me and put her finger tip on my eye. "I'm glad to see that your eye is looking better."

"I had a good doctor that works cheap." I said with a smile.

"You better wait till you get the bill!" Tom said with a laugh. I couldn't say that dinner was a total flop but it came close a time or two when Kim started asking Tom what he was up to?

Shafaun seeing Tom in hot water decided to bail him out. She turned up her beer and killed it. "Tom if you don't care, I would like another beer if you don't mind.?"

"Let's not talk business tonight." Tom said as he went to the fridge. Shafaun followed Tom to the fridge away from the others. "Thanks for the help!" Tom said as he placed two hits of LSD in her hand. "Here take one of these and give David the other one." Tom said. Shafaun put one on her tongue and washed it down with the beer she just opened.

"You have about thirty minuets before it will take full effect so you will have to go before then." "Here." Tom said as he pulled another hit of acid from his pocket and handed it to Shafaun. "Give this to David when you get him to your place."

"Is he going home with me?" Shafoun asked.

"See to that he does." Tom said as he walked off to rejoin the others.

Shafauns eyes fell upon David setting at the table. Maybe this time Tom was wasting his drugs she thought. I would have done David for free. Shafaun took two beers and sat them on the table in front of David. "Now that I've done you a favor I would like you to do me one."

"Sure! What do you want?" David agreed without knowing what she was going to ask.

"Well I need to go home in a few minutes and you know the way, so could you walk me home?" The smile that came to Davids face told his answer. "What ever she is saying to him, he sure is glad to hear it. Just look at that smile on his face." Cricket said.

Kim didn't dare let on that seeing David and Shafaun get along so well kind of made her long for the days when her and Tom got it on like that. Then she thought of when she and Cricket got it on. To think that David would have that gorgeous woman in bed by dawn was what really bothered her.

Cricket saw the look in Kim's eyes and knew what she must be thinking. How many times had Kim looked at her that way. After David and Shafaun had gone, Kim turned her attention back to Jack and her best friend Cricket.

Shafoun stopped in front of her building and handed David her key to the door. As David opened the door the hot air that had been trapped there all day hit him in the face. The night air had started to cool so when the hot air hit the cool air you could feel the difference. As he turned to let Shafoun enter first he noticed how the cool air had caused Shafauns nipples to be erect.

beside him. Her ass no sooner than hit the bed then she was on her back. A coo came from her lips as David captured her nipple between his fingertips. David placed Shafauns nipple in the warm palm and gently let his fingertips rest lightly on the globe of her breast.

"Off! Off!" Shafaun kept saying as she tugged at Davids jeans. She could tell David had an erection by the bridge in his crouch area. You could tell that David was starting to feel the effects of the hit he'd taken by the speed in which he took off his jeans and underwear and laid back down beside Shafaun. "Slow down!" Shafaun said as David took his right foot and tried to force her legs apart.

Shafoun thought at first that David didn't hear her because he went ahead and got between her legs. She was angry at first but soon realized what he was doing. David placed his erect manhood on top of Shafoun so that it laid directly over her clit. as he moved forward to kiss her nipples, his erect penis would move over her clit bringing her to full moistness. The baby soft hair on Davids chest made the nipples become erect. Shafaun gasped as Davids hot tongue pressed itself to her right nipple. By this time her hips were meeting Davids thrust with equal force. Not letting his tongue leave contact with Shafauns skin he moved to the other breast.

Shafoun tried to push her panties off while she was still lying down but could only get them part of the way off. David raised to his knees long enough to to get them the rest of the way off then returned to his place between her legs. Shafoun took her hands and placed them on Davids head and pushed it to the junction between her legs. Her pubic hair was course like a soft wire brush. David took each thumb and placed one on each side of her clit. Softly he pulled the skin open enough to where her clit was exposed to his tongue. He made little circles all around her clit with the tip of his tongue before pressing down hard on her swollen clit. Shafouns fingers dug into his hair.

"Oh God!" She cried out as she held David by the hair and thrust her hips upward. David could tell when Shafoun had finished her orgasm, she let go of his hair. She pulled him into her, slowly opened her legs like a flower to the morning sun letting him slide down between them. David had always thought of himself as well endowed, so it was a surprise when Shafoun took all of him the very first try. After a few deep thrusts David knew he was about to cum so he tried to withdraw. Each time he tried she would thrust her hips upward to recapture her prey.

David tried again to withdraw but Shafaun placed her heels behind his hips and pulled him in as far as he could go and held him. He could do nothing but let go of the load he had built up. After he finished unloading his sperm in Shafaun he collapsed on top of her sweat covered body drained and exhausted.

"Are you alright ?" Shafaun asked as she pushed him off her.

"Yes I'm doing just fine." He said as he sat up.

"Where are you going?"

"I've got to piss." He said as he fose to his feet.

"You don't have to leave tonight." She said as he walked over to the bathroom. David smiled as he told her that he wasn't going to leave just piss. They made love again after thirty minutes of rest then slept in each others arms the rest of the night.

The next morning David awoke before Shafaun and left without waking her. On his way to his room he thought of how Shafaun had held him inside her. She had to be one of the best lays he had ever had. Turning and looking at Shafauns room he knew that he would be back for more.

We had been at the commune for two months before Tom decided he had enough mushrooms for him to make enough LSD to sale. The women still didn't know what we were up to.

Shafoun and David had taken a few more trips together and was becoming quit close. Cricket was helping Kim at the clinic on a regular basis and the two of them had excepted Shafaun as a sister. Toms trips each week had stopped because of her closeness to Kim and Cricket. My wounds had healed so well that you couldn't tell I had ever been hurt.

Cricket and I shared her room. I don't think I spent more then two or three nights in the van since I got there. David and I used a big cave to grow mushrooms. Tom set up his lab in the cave too. We all thought we had it made.

Tom was showing David what to do to convert the mushrooms into acid just in case he wasn't around. He was a quick learner and caught on how to do it in no time.

"Where does Tom have you and my brother working?" Cricket asked one night after we made love.

"The mushrooms have to grow in the dark so we work in a cave not far from here." I said not thinking where this line of questioning was going.

"Why do you all act like what your doing is such a big secret if it's not illegal?" I knew right then that I had to get her mind off the subject so I climbed back on top of her and started making love to her again. It worked this time but I knew that sooner or later making love to her wasn't going to work in stopping her questions. The next morning as I started out the door to go to work, Cricket followed me out.

"Where are you going?" I asked.

"I'm going with you?" She said with a smile.

"I don't think that's a good idea." Crickets smile faded as she told me that she didn't give a damn what I thought and started leading the way. All I could do was shake my head and follow her.

David caught up with us and asked me what Cricket was doing going to work with me. I explained to him that it wasn't my idea and he above all people should know that once his sister made up her mind to do something. There was no way of stopping her.

"Where the hell do you think you are going?!" David asked as he caught up with her.

"The last time I looked at myself in the mirror I was a grown woman, little brother. I go where I want to go!" Cricket said angrily and kept walking. She stopped at the cave entrance and looked at the darkness inside. "Why is it so dark?"

"The mushrooms need to be left in the dark to grow." I said hoping she would be to afraid to go inside.

"Watch out for the snakes!" David said as he entered the cave. The word snakes made Cricket stop dead in her tracks. That was the one thing she hadn't thought of. Cricket wasn't afraid of the dark but she was deeply afraid of snakes. "Come on in." He said as he got far enough inside to where Cricket couldn't see him.

"Fuck this shit!" Crickett said as she turned around and headed back. David came back out after she had left. "Boy that was close."

"That was to close!" I said as we both watched as she headed back down the path without turning around. Tom thought it was funny when we told him what happened later that day.

"You should be proud of him Jack." Tom said patting David on the shoulder. "Not only did he quite Cricketts suspissions but he made it to where she won't be in any hurry to come back up here."

I was just hoping that Cricket would stop asking me questions that I didn't want to answer. I thought to myself. The rest of the day went by without any problems. When I did get home, Cricket was telling me about the talk she had with Kim. Kim had been telling her about the kinds of snakes she could find around here. She had advised her to stay out of the woods and she wouldn't have to worry about snakes. "You should do what Kim said." I told her.

After two days Tom had made enough LSD to get the whole commune stoned. Tom had taken a pen and made little dots on sheets of paper. Then he had me and David take the eye dropper and touch it to each dot. Once that we had done that he had us take scissors and cut out each little dot of acid. As we were leaving he handed David two dots and told him to give them to Shafaun. "Tell her not to take more then one. This is a knew batch and I don't know how strong it is yet."

"I'll probably take the other one just to be sure." David said with a little laugh.

"Well if you both take them at the same time, you'll end up fucking each others brains out!" Tom told him as we left the cave.

Shafaun had grilled two stakes and baked potatoes. David was making good money and wanted to be a big spender. Anything that her wanted it had to be the best. She had never been around what seemed an endless supply of money so she made the best of it because she knew how soon things could change. Was she really falling for David or was it his money? She hadn't been with another man since the first night with David. To tell the truth she din't want to be with anyone else. Tom had stopped dropping by for sex since David moved in and she was glad of that. Most of the colored people around her had accepted David and the ones that didn't left him alone because he was Toms friend.

The people she sold drugs to couldn't care less. Davids sister came by to see her this morning, telling her that David was working in a cave full of snakes. "I'm sure David is safe as long as he has Jack with him." She told Shafaun.

The sound of the spring being pulled on the screen door as it opened brought her attention back to the door. David came through the door with a smile and a kiss. He started to tell Shafaun about Cricket and what had happened this morning but she told him she had talked to Cricket and knew all about it.

"Well here is something you don't know about." He said patting his shirt pocket.

"You found us some pot!" She exclaimed with excitement.

"No something better." He said pulling the LSD out of his pocket.

"I've fixed us a good supper so we will eat before we take the acid."

"Tom said not to take more then one hit." David said as he laid them down on the table. Oh Tom's getting tight in his old age. She thought to herself.

"I've been taking as many as two or three hits at one time." She said.

"Well he said that he didn't know how strong this batch is, so don't take more then one hit, okay?"

"Okay I can live with that." Shafaun said with a laugh. After the two of them had eaten they sat back on the bed and put the hits of acid on their tongues and washed them down with a beer. David turned to his favorite station on the radio and laid back to enjoy his buzz. Shafaun thought it would take thirty minutes for the acid to take effect. It frightened her when it only took five minutes to feel its effect.

"This must be some good shit." David said as his forehead broke out into a sweat. He hadn't taken acid enough that he could tell if it was working right or not. Shafaun had.

She knew that she shouldn't be feeling like she was. Her heart was pounding like a drum and she was having a hard time moving her arms and legs. Panic set in when her whole body became numb and she felt like the only thing that worked was her mind.

All she could do was lay there and watch as the exspression on Davids face told her he was in deep trouble. His eyes were bugged out and his mouth was open as wide as he could get it so he could breath. Shafaun wanted to run and get Kim to help them but she couldn't move. Tears ran from her eyes as she watched David take his last breath. She knew she would join him soon.

The next morning I waited for David to come out so we could go to work but he didn't come out. I walked up and tapped on the screen door but I didn't hear a sound from inside. Thinking that they had fucked all night like Tom had said. I thought they must still be asleep. I opened the screen door and entered. They were fully dressed and sitting up in bed dead.

"My God! What is going on here?" I said out loud even knowing they were dead. The acid Tom gave David yesterday! I thought as I ran out of the room.

Tom was going to take that load to Nashville this morning. I said to myself as I ran to stop him. When I got to Kim's house I could see that Toms truck was gone. "Where is Tom?" I asked Kim when she came to the door.

"He's gone to Nashville for some medical supplies.!" She said. "What is wrong Jack?"

"It's Shafaun and David, they are dead!"

"Are you kidding?!" Kim asked not wanting to believe what she just heard. Without saying another word Kim went back inside and grabbed up her medical bag and ran to where David and Shafaun lay.

I watched as Kim froze in her tracks as she looked upon a horrible sight. Both David and Shafaun lay with their eyes and mouths open as if the last thing they saw was a frightening sight. There was no doubt that they were dead and had been for some time. Kim turned to me and demanded that I tell her what I knew about this.

"This is the way I found them, I swear it!" Kim could tell that there was more to that story that I wasn't telling.

"Why were you looking for Tom when you came up to me?"

"Well Tom runs this place and I knew he would want to contact the law."

"What's Tom got that the law would want?" As Kim turned back to where David and Shafaun lay she thought of how Tom had always tried to make money by selling drugs. "What kind of drugs is he selling?" Kim asked as she turned back to me.

"LSD." I said. "He made up about five thousand hits from the mushrooms."

"Now Jack this is important. Do you know how many hits they took?"

"Yes Tom gave them one hit apiece."

"My God! He has five thousand hits of certain death with him." Kim screamed as she ran out the door and headed for a phone. I knew Kim was going to call the law and that they would be here in a little while. I had to be gone before they got here.

How was I going to tell Cricket that her brother and his girlfriend were dead and that I can't stay around to tell anyone what I know about it."Thanks for the ride." I said as I left them and headed to where Cricket was still sleeping. Should I just gather my things and go or wake her to tell her that her brother was dead. I knew all about the drugs. I bent and kissed her forehead. Cricket smiled but didn't wake up. "Thanks for the love." I said then walked out the door with my things. I caught a ride to where the state road crossed the interstate and got off there. I had no longer gotten out of the truck then the Tenn. State police came by as fast as he dared to go. I would like to have stayed and help Cricket through this but I couldn't take the chance that they were looking for me.

The heat waves coming off the black top highway blurred my vision. As I took the back of my hand and wiped the salty sweat from my eyes I caught a glimps of the old rust colored truck coming straight at me. What in hell is wrong with this son of a bitch? I ask myself as he didn't seem to slow down. There was a bank behind me but it was at least fifteen feet straight up. I had to chose to climb the hill or get run over by the truck I chose to climb.

I don't know how I did it but I got to the top of the hill about the time the old truck sputtered and died to a stop. If you think I made it up that hill fast, you should have seen me come down it! I was standing by the old mans window in about five steps. When I saw the drunk old man behind the wheel I just got angrier. "I should drag your ass out of that truck and kick your ass!"

"Now you wouldn't want to hit an old man who stopped to give you a ride?" He said with a grin.

"Old man, you just about killed me!"

"No I wasn't trying to kill you young man! I was just giving you a ride." Before the old man could get out another word he started to vomit out the truck window. The vomit glanced off the truck door and splattered my shoes. My eyes flashed with anger. I had lived with a drunk my whole life my whole life not to know one when I saw him.

"Give me a ride! You drunk bastard, I wouldn't ride ten feet with you!"

"Well young man you drive and I'll hitch a ride." He replied then laughed. Still laughing the old man reached under the seat and pulled out a half pint of gin. "Get in boy and lets get going." He said as he moved to the passenger seat. At first I wasn't going to get in and drive until I saw the county police car coming toward us.

"Well come on boy! We don't have all day!"

"Jack Benson is my name, not boy." I said as I got behind the wheel.

"Ben Tall is my name." The old man said between drinks.

"Well, Ben Tall. How far is it to the next town?" I asked as I pulled the old truck back on the highway.

"It's about fifteen miles to Greenville but I'm not going that far. I live about ten miles from here." Ben said as he looked out his door window. "Them black and gray clouds mean we are about to have a big storm." Pointing to the east.

"You will need to show me where to turn off." I said as we drove.

"Just stay on this road until you get to a pair of red wagon wheels and turn there." Ben replied in blurred speech. I reached the driveway in about ten minutes but Ben had passed out cold.

The sign above the road read Tall Pines Plantation. I was surprised that the house was so far from the main road. The dust coming off the driveway was so thick that I couldn't see anything behind me. It seemed strange to me that a man who owned a plantation couldn't at least put gravel on his driveway.

Just as the old truck topped the hill I could see that there was a two story mansion in front of me. It had big white columns that held up a balcony that went all the way down the front of the house. As the truck came to a stop the dust cloud that had been following us caught up. The cloud filled the cab leaving me and Ben covered in red dust. The sound of the screen door slamming shut brought my attention the the front porch. Just as I got the truck door open I saw her standing on the porch.

Sandy had seen the old truck come across the bridge at a high rate of speed and was sure that there was something wrong with her pa. As many times as her pa came home drunk or sober he would not park like that. The young man who was getting out of the truck sure wasn't her pa. This man was what she had been praying for.

He stood five foot ten and weighed almost two hundred pounds. Even with his cloths on she could tell that there was no fat there. Sandy walked around the truck without taking her eyes off of me. When she did she saw Ben laying passed out in the truck seat covered in red dust she burst out in laughter. Sandy stuck her arm through the window and shook Ben's arm. "PA get up!" She kept saying as she shook his arm.

"He's out cold." I said as I came around the truck to join her.

"Could you help me get him inside to his bed?"

"Sure!" I said without hesitation. "I'll take the heavy top and you take the legs." When I opened the truck door Ben almost fell out into my arms. "Angle if you will lead the way." I said not knowing her name.

"What did you call me?"

"Angle."

"My mother use to call me that." Sandy told me as she grabbed Ben's feet and headed up the steps. I could tell this wasn't the first time she had done this. Sandy turned her back to me and between Ben's ankles lead the way. She lead us through a long hallway to the second door to the right. By the time we reached the big four poster bed, I was ready to put Ben down. After we got Ben put to bed I turned to see Sandy tip toeing out of the room.

"You could have run a horse through there and Ben wouldn't have woken up."

"I'm Sandy Tall." She said as she reached out to shake my hand.

"Jack Benson." I said as I took her hand in mine. Sandy's hand was rough and calloused from hard work.

"Glad to meet you." We both said about the same time.

"Well Jack I have made a big supper for me and pa so you must at least eat his supper for your kindness. I won't take no for an answer."

"Miss Sandy Tall, I would be glad to have supper with you but I would like to wash up first." I said as I saw my reflection in the mirror.

"Right this way." Sandy said as she lead me this time down a different hall and up a flight of stairs. The bathroom had three doors to it. One went to the bedroom on the right and the other door on the left went to a bedroom too. The third door went to the hallway. Set in the middle of the floor was an old eagle claw tub.

"I'll just run out to the truck and get my bag." I told her.

"While your doing that I'll run you some bath water." Sandy said as I left the room. I took more notice of the house as I went to the truck to get my stuff. I could see pictures of black men, women, and children that covered both wall down the hallway. In a big picture with a brass tag that read 'Prime one' was a man with cotton white hair and beard.

"He was my great great grand dad the first." The voice from behind me said.

"First what?"

"First breeding stock he bought for this plantation."

"Well I could tell that it wasn't a family picture." I said with a smile.

"All these others are his kids so you could say it was family." Sandy said without a smile. I couldn't believe what Sandy had just said. All the people were his kids.

"You mean he fathered all these people?"

"They all can take thier roots to him. I was just coming to see if you got lost in this big old house." Sandy said.

"No, I'm not lost. I was just looking at the pictures."

"My grandfather use to do the same thing." Sandy said with her eyes locked on me as I stood there. "Sometimes he would stand in the hallway and talk to these pictures for hours. He would tell each one how much his dad had paid for him or her. Depending on who he happened to be talking to at the time." At least that's what her grandpa had told her one time. "Now you take prime there." Sandy said pointing toward the picture. "He was bought down south somewhere and he cost two thousand dollars."

"Your grandpa must have really liked him a lot to pay that much." I said not knowing what the fuck I was talking about.

"Yeah! He was his first stud they bought for here."

"Do you mean that your grandpa sold and breed people like cattle?" I asked with surprise.

"Sure he did. That's how this place worked. You put your prime stud to the wenches and when they had a sucker, you sold it to buy more prime stock." Sandy said. I didn't say that I agreed to what they did, but to them it was the way they made their living.

"I'm not judging you for what your grandparents did." I said as I moved down the hall.

"While your taking your bath, I'll set the food on the table." Sandy said as she headed for the dinning room. After setting the table, Sandy sat down in one of the chairs. "Do you think pa had listened to her the last time she told him ' If he didn't get her some help around here that she was going to leave and he would have to do it all himself'. Pa had never done her a good deal since her mother died so what made her think he would now.

"Do you really think pa hired Jack to go to work on the farm?" She asked herself.

"Well I'm not asleep and that is a good looking young man up there in that tub. He brought his clothes." Sandy gave a little squeale as she thought about it.

I stripped off my dirty clothes and climbed in the warm bathwater Sandy had fixed for me. I had to admit it felt pretty good to get in some warm water. when a man is on the road he gets tired of taking his baths in creeks. "Jack old boy, you had better take advantage of this while you can." I told myself. I had looked at the sky when I went to the truck to get my things. And from the looks of those gray clouds, it would be raining in about an hour or so. "Go ahead and let it rain." I said as I slide under the water. If I play my cards right. I may get to stay awhile.

Sandy put away the dishes that she and Ben had always used and put out the one's that her mother got from her mother. It seemed to her that Jack liked old things and these dishes was at least a hundred years old. The thought of having someone to share the work around this place made her feel good. What ever it took to keep Jack here, she made up her mind, that she would do.

She thought of going up to the bathroom and asking Jack if there was anything he needed but he might take that the wrong way. Sandy could hear Jack's foot steps come down the hallway to the kitchen. "Dam he's good looking." She said out loud before she realized it.

"So are you!" I said as I came to a stop at the dinning table.

"You be seated and I'll bring you something to drink. Would you like milk, water or beer?" Sandy asked. "Pa brought some beer a while back but never drank any of it. He drinks gin and once he starts he don't stop till he passes out."

"That's the first thing I noticed about your pa." I said trying to make fun of his drinking.

"I didn't do a good job of it because." The grin folded from Sandy's face.

"Beer!" I said. "I'll have a beer!" I told Sandy as I sat down in a chair. I looked at all the food that was on the table and could tell that this wasn't an everyday meal. "I'm sorry if I interrupted some special get together." I said as Sandy returned to the table with my beer.

"It's just something I do each year to remember the last day I spent with my mom before she died." Sandy said as she sat down. "I was hoping pa would come home and share it with me but as you can see he started drinking early this morning. To tell the truth I'm glad he's not here to spoil it for me."

Not knowing if Ben had brought Jack here to work. Sandy thought she would ask a few questions. Sandy asked me where I was from.

"I was born on a mountain top in Kentucky. My dad always said we got the morning sun two hours before anyone else." I said with a laugh.

"That must be a hell of a hill." Sandy said. "Why did you leave?" Sandy asked not realizing that I went pail with fear from the question.

After I got the fear under control. "To see the world."

"How did my pa meet you to hire you to work here?" Sandy asked.

"Wait a minute Sandy. Your pa didn't hire me to work here. I met him when he picked me up hitching a ride. The first time I saw your pa I thought he was going to run me over. I was about to punch him out but the gin beat me to it!"

"It seems that every time we talk about pa one of us gets mad." Sandy said. "From here on out we won't talk about pa."

"That sounds great to me!" I said trying to put Ben out of my mind. The rest of the meal was spent in small talk. After we finished eating Sandy started telling me of how I was going to hire me to work for them and make her pa think he had.

"I'm sure the good Lord will forgive me for this one lie."

The sound of the lightning striking near by brought both me and Sandy out of our chairs. "Dam that was close!" Sandy said as we ran for the door. The rain started coming down so hard that it was hard to see more then a few hundred feet away.

"It doesn't look like you will be going anywhere tonight." Sandy said as she closed the door. She walked me back up the stairs to where my things sat in the bathroom. Once I got my things she lead me to the bedroom across from hers. There was a big antique bed with four big posts with cupids carved on them. There was a night stand beside the bed with a pipe stand on it. As I looked at the pipe it reminded me that I was out of ciggerrets.

"By any chance do you or your father smoke?"

"I don't smoke and pa only smokes a pipe once in a while. We can go down stairs and you can smoke his pipe if you like." Once we got to the sitting room She gave me the pipe and a pouch of what she called tobacco.

When I opened the pouch it seemed it wasn't tobacco in it. "This isn't tobacco!"

"It's what he's been smoking for years. He grows it himself." Sandy told me.

I knew exactly what was in the pouch by the smell. I picked a bud out of the pouch and crumbled it into the pipe. It was so dry that the bud turned to dust. Sandy watched as I fired up the pipe and took a long draw on it. The pot was so strong that I started coughing after two hits.

"It must be some strong stuff." Sandy said trying to hold back her laughter and failed. The pot took effect almost at once as I sat down in the chair. She noticed how the smoke had made my eyes glass over and they looked like to blue marbles. "Are you alright?" She asked with a smile.

"Yes I'm alright but I would be better with another beer."

"I can fix that problem!" Sandy said as she left and went to get the beer. I was lighting the pipe again as Sandy came back with the beer. "I don't know how that pipe will effect you, but if it's anything like pa. It's going to put you to sleep."

"I can handle it!" I assured her and hit it again and took the beer she offered.

"Well what do you say?" Sandy asked.

"Thank you!" I said thinking she wanted me to thank her for the beer.

"No! I mean will you stay and work for me and pa." Sandy added.

"I told you he didn't say anything to me about working here."

"I know that. You know that but pa don't know that." She told me with a smile. "I'll hire you and when pa wakes up he will think that he hired you. In the morning when pa wakes up he won't remember what he did today. Believe me he will think it was all his idea and pat himself on the back."

"Yes! I'll work for you and you can tell Ben anything you want." By the time I finished the beer, I was feeling no pain. The pot I had smoked was coursing through my veins causing my head to spin like a top. When Sandy looked at me she had that 'I told you so look on her face.

"Do you need help to your room?" Sandy asked as she reached out her hand to help me from my chair. After telling Sandy how I could hold my beer and pot, I wasn't about to ask her for her help to bed. I lead the way to my room the best I could without falling.

I never turned around but I knew Sandy was walking behind me with a big grin on her face. She had stopped her grinning as she left me at my door. My eyes were fixed on the big high bed across the room and headed for it.

I no sooner lay down on my back when the whole room started spinning. I could feel the beer I just drank starting to come back up. I knew I had to get up fast or I would have a wet bed that smelled like beer for the night. I found that the room was going faster then before once I got to my feet. The first thing I noticed was that there were three doors in front of me when I got the room to slow down enough that I could see.

I wonder which one is the bathroom door? I ask myself as I felt the sour taste reach my mouth. I just hope this is the right one! I thought as I turned the knob. I fell to my knees in front of the porcelain God and gave him his tribute. Once I had finished both doors were shut and I just grabbed the first one I came to. As I pulled the door open I stood there in shock.

Sandy was standing there in the nude with her back to me. She was facing a full length mirror. The night gown she was putting on lay on her shoulders and her head wasn't through the hole yet. Her firm breast and private part were easily seen in the mirror. My mind told me that I should get back to my room before she sees me but her beauty held me in a trance.

I finally convinced my legs to move and thought I had gotten by with her not seeing me. You pick a hell of a time to get sick. I told myself on the way back to my room.

Sandy had noticed Jack as he came through the door. At first she was a little frightened but when he backed out without making a sound proved to her that it was an accident. She also knew that she had held up the gown a lot longer then it usually took.

I wonder why I like the way it makes me feel when a man see's me nude? Sandy asked herself as she lay down. I wonder what Jack would look like in the nude? She asked herself as she placed a hand on her right breast. Jack Benson was the first young man sandy had seen in two years and if nothing else she was going to think about him while she masterbaited tonight.

Sandy's right hand found it's way down her stomach to her mound. I wonder what he would be like? She asked herself as her fingers found their way to the junction of her legs. She had a hot flash when she was finally able to picture Jack in the nude. Sandy couldn't believe how wet the back of her gown had gotten. She could feel it on her ass. The rest of the night Sandy slept with Jack on her mind and her hand on her mound.

At five o'clock the next morning Ben stuck his head through Sandy's bedroom door and was telling her to get up and fix him some breakfast. Sandy's head jerked as she thought of Jack asleep in the other room. "I'll bet pa doesn't even know Jack is even here."

Sandy went in and sat down on the toilet before she noticed that Jacks door was all the way open. There he lay sound asleep with the cover thrown on the floor. Jack was naked except for a pair of brief underwear. Sandy took the back of her hand and rubbed her eyes. This was the first time she had ever seen a man in briefs. Could she sneak into his room and get a better look at him without waking him up? Sandy stopped at Jacks door Just to make sure he was asleep. As slow as a snail She walked across the room.

After she reached the bed Sandy stood looking down at Jacks naked body. Sandy let out a loud gasp as her eyes looked upon a fully erect penis in the morning. Jacks erection was about the size of a walking stick she often used to drive the cows in for milking. Jacks movement brought Sandy's attention back to Jacks head. His eyes were closed but Sandy could feel his eyes on her. Just as she started to go back to the bathroom, Ben called from the hallway for her to get to the kitchen.

As Sandy reached the bathroom she closed the door and gave a sigh of relief. Now to go see how much of yesterday her pa could remember. Sandy notices that Ben had his back to her as he fixed a pot of coffee.

"What were you doing up there?" He asked without turning around.

"I was using the bathroom is all." Sandy replied. "Oh papa, thank you so much!" She walked up behind him and threw her arms around his waist. Ben had no idea what she was talking about. But this was the first time his daughter had given him a hug in two years.

"What in sam hell are you talking about girl?"

"For hiring that nice young man up stairs !" Sandy replied.

"I didn't hire anyone so where did you get the idea that I did?"

"From that young man you hired." Sandy repeated.

"I don't remember hiring him."

"Well I'm not surprised! You don't remember telling me that you was going to get me some help around here do you?"

"Yes I remember telling you that but that was a week ago." Ben had to admit he didn't remember much about yesterday.

"By the time that young man got you home you were already passed out. Jack Benson said you hired him right before you ran off the road, so he drove you home safely."

Ben wasn't sure if he picked that young man up before or after he had ran off the road. He must have hired him because he was upstairs. "Well if I hired him why isn't he down here ready for work?" He asked looking towards the stairs.

"I'll go get him up and fix us a big breakfast to start the day." Sandy stood in the doorway before she walked over to the bed. She gave Jack the once over before she said anything.

"Jack it's time to get up and go down to breakfast." Sandy said as she gently poked me on the shoulder. "Pa wants to meet you!" She said as she more forcefully poked my arm. Sandy's eyes went straight to my morning erection. "I wonder if it stays like that?" She asked out loud before she could get her hand to her mouth to stop herself.

"No it doesn't!" I said as her eyes came back to my now open eyes. Sandy could feel her face turn red even in the darkened room. As I watched her I could see her mouth move but there wasn't a sound coming out.

"You were just playing opossum wasn't you?" Sandy said when she did get her voice back. "It's plain to see that you are awake now." she said as she left the room.

"First things first." I said as I jumped from the bed and hurried to the bathroom.

"I did tell him that we start working at five didn't I?" Ben asked when Sandy came back in the kitchen.

"I'm sure you did pa. He will be right down." Sandy was pleased when I walked into the kitchen and sat down. "Jack Benson, this is my pa Ben Tall." She said trying to keep things as business like as she could.

"You may have told me yesterday Jack Benson but have you ever worked on a cattle ranch before?"

"No I haven't worked on a cattle ranch before but I have worked on a horse ranch in Kentucky before." I told Ben. "There shouldn't be to much difference."

"You mean you and your pa raised racing horses?" Ben asked.

"No! I said that I worked on a horse ranch. My pa never worked anywhere."

Ben sensed that he hit a soft spot and decided to let it drop. After all the young man looked fit enough to do the work Sandy was doing by herself. "Around here we start work at six. You will get a hundred a week plus room and board. Sandy knows what needs to be done around here. So you will take your orders from her." Ben turned to Sandy and told her. "See I told you I would get some help around here."

Sandy looked at me with a smile of her own and told Ben "Thank you pa!" Than gave me a wink. Sandy watched as Ben and Jack walked out the screen door letting it slam behind them. The hard rain from the night had made mud holes all over the place. Where there wasn't a mud hole there was thick mud. It stuck to our feet like brick mortar. Not knowing what Ben had in mind to start with, I followed him as he went straight to the old truck.

At first I didn't know what he was doing until he raised the truck seat and pulled out an empty bottle of gin. "Shit fire!" Ben said as he threw the empty bottle down. Ben looked at his watch then at me. "I'm going to show you the wagon and you will need to stack the hay on it." Ben said as he headed towards the barn. After we reached where the hay was stored. Ben told me that the wagon was out there, that the hay went on. Pointing to a door that lead back out side.

Ben walked over to where the hay was stacked and pulled a half empty bottle of gin from behind the bail of hay. "You will need to put about fifty bails on the wagon." He said as he turned up the bottle and emptied it in two swallows. After he had finished the bottle he told me that he was going into town for supplies. I knew what he meant by supplies but I didn't say anything. The door was on a spring so you didn't have to put the bail down to open it.

As I came through the door I stopped in my tracks. The wagon Ben had told me was out there was out there in a field about two hundred yards away. It wasn't the kind of wagon you pulled with a tractor. It was the kind you pulled with a mule.

"We'll just use old Jake like I've been doing since the tractor broke down."

"Who is Jake?" I asked as we headed to the stables.

"Jake is our mule, he has been around this place for thirty years or better. He is old but he still can pull a wagon." Sandy had dropped back so I would be walking in front of her. She was watching my ass as we walked. I could feel her eyes on me but I didn't know she was looking at my ass.

"Where to?" I ask as we reached the stables.

"What?" Sandy asked not knowing what I said. "Oh this way!" She said as she took the lead and opened the door to the tack room. "We'll need that and that and those." Sandy pointing to the harness and the lead reins. A smile crossed my face as I thought of telling Sandy that I knew what we would need but decided to play along. Jake the old mule had his head stuck out of his stall watching me pack the harness towards him.

"Old man are you ready to do the same work today?" Sandy asked as she reached out to rub his nose. It seemed to me that Jake could understand every word she said cause he backed up in his stall until she opened the stall door. Sandy stood out side the stall to see if I could put the harness on Jake.

"This is night storm." Sandy said as I came out of Jake's stall leading Jake. She was standing by a beautiful black horse with a white blaze down her face. I watched as Sandy reached into a bag of oats setting by the stall door and pulled out a handful.

"Storm was born on a stormy night. He has a lot of spirit so I'm the only one that he will let ride him."

"I wasn't thinking of taking him for a ride." I said as I lead Jake to the

"You can talk to me Jack Benson. You can at least do that." I continued walking without saying a word. "You can be quiet if you want to but I'm going to do the talking for both of us."

"The whole idea of hiring you was so I could have someone to talk to. Is there some reason you don't like talking about yourself?" Sandy asked not expecting an answer.

"No!" I said without looking at her.

"Well I can't make you talk but you can't make me shut up either. So that makes us kind of even doesn't it?"

"If you say so but if you want my opinion we should leave the past behind us because I live for today every day." Sandy couldn't believe I had spoken with a full sentence.

"You talk up a storm when you do start talking." Sandy said with a big 'I win' smile on her face. As we came around a bend the old plantation house came into view. It was two story house that had vines growing up the sides that covered the first floor. Most of the top of the house had been on fire that left the logs a charcoal black.

"What caused the fire?"

"Well it can talk." Sandy said with a smile. I couldn't help but smile too.

"What about the fire?" I ask again.

"Well my great grandma set it on fire back in the 1800's. I was told that she caught my great grandpa fucking a wench who worked in the kitchen and great grandma set the place on fire."

"Didn't your great grandma know this was a stud plantation?"

"Sure she knew that this was a breeding plantation but this happened ten years years after the civil war." Sandy said with a laugh. I just sat and looked at the old house as Sandy went on with the story.

I could picture in my mind how mad Sandy's great grandma was to find her husband making love to a slave girl. The wagon wheel on my side hit a deep rut and threw me and Sandy together It threw Sandy almost in my lap. I captured Sandy in a bear hug before she was thrown out of the wagon. My right arm went around her waist as I grabbed the seat with my left hand. By the time Sandy stopped falling her breast were resting on my forearm. I could tell from the feel of her breast on my arm that she wasn't wearing a bra.

"Are you alright?" I ask from behind her. still holding her in my right arm.

"Yes I'm alright!" Sandy said as she moved back onto the seat. Jake stopped as he came to the gate that lead us into the pasture.

"I'll get the gate Sandy said as she jumped down from the wagon. The old rusty hinges made a high pitched screech when it swung open. Without being told Jake started walking again as soon as the gate was open enough for him to proceed.

"We'll leave that open while we are here." Sandy said as she climbed back into the seat. I noticed that the top two buttons on her shirt was missing as she climbed back on the wagon. Sandy's young breast pushed at the tight fitting shirt to spread open. As soon as Sandy saw what I was looking at she pinched the shirt together with her fingers. I didn't want to emberass her so I turned my head.

"It must have busted the buttons off when we hit that hole. Would you like to have my shirt?" I asked without looking at her.

"I guess the first thing we must do to work together is start showing that we trust each other." Sandy said as she let the shirt fall open. It felt good to think that Sandy trusted me. Even though I hadn't done anything for her not to trust me. It still felt good.

As soon as the cows saw the wagon load of hay they started mooing and walking towards us."Stop here Jake!" Sandy said as we came to a circle fence. "We need to take the strings off the bails and put them over there." She said pointing towards the fence.

By the time I got down from the wagon, Sandy had already taken a bail off the wagon and cut the strings. As Sandy would reach down and grab a pleat of hay her shirt would open enough to flash her tits. I had told myself that I wasn't going to get sexually involved with Sandy and I had kept it strictly business for a whole hour and a half.

As I pulled one of the bails off the wagon Jake started walking towards the lake. I started to run to catch him. Sandy grabbed my arm and told me he was just going to get him a drink. "The old man deserves at least that."

"There is a place we can sit and wait for Jake!" Sandy was pointing to a moss covered hill. The tree's that stood there gave us all kinds of shade. Sandy had simply stopped trying to keep her shirt closed.

"Pa told me that someday this place would be mine. When it is I'm going to build my house right here. Look out over the bottom land that lay before us."

"It's kind of a long way from the road isn't it?" I ask.

"Yes it is and that's what I like about it." As we sat and talked the wind changed direction and I thought I could smell a skunk.

"We should find a different place to sit because a skunk has been here before us." I said as I rose to my feet. Sandy's laughter stunned me to say the least. "Whats so funny?"

"It's not a skunk that smells like that. It's that plant!" She said pointing toward a large plant. "That is what you smoked last night." I walked over to the plant and pulled a bud off. The pot plant stood about ten feet tall and the buds where so heavy that they pulled the limbs to the ground.

"This place was covered with different kinds of pot plants. They grow wild here so pa just lets it grow."

"Don't you know what this is Sandy?"

"Yes they are hemp plants that grandpa grew for rope back in WW1."

"Who all knows about this!?"

"Just me and pa as far as I know."

"This stuff is worth a lot of money when it's cut and dried!" I told her.

"How come?"

"Well I know a lot of people that would pay one hundred dollars a pound." Sandy just looked at me like I was crazy.

By the time we got back to the house it was ten in the morning. The sun had got so hot that the ground was starting to dry up. After putting Jake back into his stall. Sandy and I went to the house. I sat down at the table while Sandy went upstairs to change her shirt. When she came back down I was still sitting at the table drinking a cup of coffee.

"You don't have to drink that cold coffee Jack. I'll make you a fresh pot."

"No! That's alright. I'm use to cold coffee and hot beer." I said with a laugh. Sandy didn't say anymore. She just went to the stove and started to fix our dinner.

"I wonder where pa is?" Sandy said more to herself then to me. "He is probably in some bar drunk by now." Answering her own question. Not knowing what to say to her. I just sat there drinking my coffee.

"I guess it's for the best. If he was here he'd just be in the way." I tried to get her mind off of him by talking about her love life.

"How long has it been since you went out on a date?" I could see from her expression that my question came as a surprise.

"I don't have time for such foolishness." Sandy replied.

"As pretty as you are I would think that you would have boys coming here all the time."

"Well the only boyfriend I've ever had was back in school. And all he wanted was to get in my pants."

"I'm sorry I asked. I had no right to get into your personal life. All I ever did was go from one girl to another trying to fuck them. I can see why he wanted you." I said more to myself then to Sandy, but she heard me.

"You say what your thinking, don't you?"

"Life is to short to waste time pretending you don't know what you want, when you really do."

"What about your love life?" Sandy asked as we sat down to eat.

"I had a girlfriend once. We lost contact a few months back."

"Then you haven't been with anybody for a good while?"

"It's hard to find love when you are on the road like I am."

"We had better get back to work." Sandy said as she got up from the table and walked to the door. We went to the tack room and got out two saddles.

I put one on Jake and she put one on Storm. Jake didn't care what you put on him as long as you gave him a handful of oats.

Storm was a different matter. He was living up to his name. He was so jumpy that I was afraid he would throw Sandy. "Don't you think we should hook Jake back up to the wagon and leave Storm here?"

"I think I can handle him!" Sandy said as she slung her leg over Storms back. "He will calm down after we get going."

"Your the boss." I said as I climbed on Jake.

"I don't want you to think of me as your boss. I would rather you thought of me as a partner."

"Well wait up partner!" I said as she done had Storm in a full trot. I was still sitting there as Sandy and Storm ran through the field.

"Come on Jake! We can't let her run off and leave us like this!" I kept saying as I kicked Jake in the flanks with my heels. Sandy was watching from across the field with a smile on her face.

"Just let Jake go! He knows the way!" Sandy shouted from across the field. As I stopped kicking Jake, he took off in a slow walk. As Jake and I caught up with Sandy and Storm. Storm bolted and ran for the trees.

Jake simply walked to the other side of the road. What had caused this ruckus was a five foot diamond back on the other side of the road. Jake wouldn't leave the road that he walked so many times before. I started to kick Jake in the flanks again. I pulled his head to the direction that I wanted him to go and I kicked with all the power my legs could make. He finally got going towards Storm and Sandy. He did speed up a little. I couldn't tell if Sandy was in control of Storm because we were so far behind. All I knew was the last time I saw her she looked to be in trouble.

"Woo! Woo!" Sandy cried as she pulled on the reins to get Storm to stop. Storm darted under some low hanging branches and carried Sandy with him. The first limb knocked Sandy backward on Storms back. The second limb caught Sandy's shirt and skinned her like a squiarl. The shirt caught on the limb and pulled Sandy off of Storms back.

I was off Jake before he even stopped. Sandy was sitting up by the time I had reached her. "Are you hurt?" I knelt down beside her.

"I think so!" She replied as she rubbed her head. It had left a big bump the size of an egg.

"I'm going to get Jake and take you back to the house." I told Sandy as I ran to get Jake. I must have noticed that Sandy was nude from the waist up before she did.

At first she thought her fore arm over her breast trying to hide them. "That's the second shirt I've lost today." Sandy said as she took the arm she was using to cover herself out to me so I could give her a hand up. After helping Sandy off the ground, I took off my shirt and gave it to her.

"Thank you!" Sandy said as she put the shirt on. She didn't bother to button it up. Sandy sat in the saddle and road while I walked ahead of Jake. "I want you to know that this doesn't happen everyday." Sandy said from Jake's back.

"I guess what I'm trying to say Jack, is that I don't want you to leave me. I need your help so please don't quite."

"I'll try it for a little while." I told her with a smile. As soon as we came upon Storm he walked straight up to Sandy, stuck his nose to her pocket and snorted. "I don't think you deserve any oats, do you?" Sandy said as she petted Storm on the neck.

I came to Storms defense by telling Sandy that it was a snake that spooked him. "Well in that case, I guess you can have at least one handful of oats." Sandy climbed back on Storm and headed for home. by the time I reached the barn with Jake, Sandy had already unsaddled Storm and gone to the house.

I went to the house as soon as I got Jake put up. Sandy had already took off my shirt and put on a t-shirt with a funny logo on it. The shirt showed three wolves standing around little red riding hood standing in a fire. The caption said ' nothing brings out the wolves like a bitch in heat'.

Once we finished milking the cows, we were both ready to go and sit down and rest. Just as we were entering the back door, Ben pulled up in the truck. I could tell by the way he was slumped over the wheel that he was drunk again. As I started to go to the truck Sandy yelled at me to stop.

"Let the old bastard be!" Sandy tried to mask the hurt but couldn't her tears. As we entered the kitchen I noticed that I had gone all day without a ciggerret.

"Whats wrong?" Sandy asked as she watched me feel my pockets.

"I never went and got me any smokes."

"Well I can't drive and pa ain't in no shape to drive you to the store. You can smoke pa's pipe if you want." The idea of smoking that pipe wasn't my first choice but it was all that I had.

After going to the sitting room and getting the pipe. I could tell that there was still pot left in it from the night before. I put the stem to my mouth and lit the bowl. The way the bowl was packed made it hard to draw through. Once the smoke reached my lungs it caused me to start coughing. I thought of the time I smoked with Cricket and her telling me to take a drink of beer before taking a hit off the pipe. I decided to go back to the kitchen and get a beer. By the time I got back to the kitchen, Sandy already had me a beer on the table.

I was already feeling the effects of the pot and almost missed the chair as I sat down.

"What's wrong with you?" Sandy asked me as I grinned.

"I would say that I'm stoned."

"Your eyes look like glass marbles."

"It's because I've been smoking."

"Your blue eyes look like two pools of water in the dessert." Sandy said with a big smile. The sound of the screen door being pulled open told us that Ben had finally made it to the house.

Sandy met him at the door so he couldn't get out of hearing what she had to say. "And just where do you think your going?" Sandy asked just as Ben stepped through the door.

"Now don't be like that sissy." Ben said in a drunken slur. "I promise that tomorrow I hire you some help. I promise." Ben kept saying as he tried to get away from Sandy.

"You hired Jack Benson yesterday, you drunk fool!" Sandy yelled at Ben. "Your so drunk you don't even remember."

"Just give him a few days he'll work out." Ben said as he stumbled to his bed.

"I wish I could drive." Sandy said "I would buy a car and let that old man have this fucking place."

It was the first time I had heard Sandy say a curse word. Being as high as I was I started laughing.

"What's so damn funny Mr. Benson?" Sandy asked in a loud voice.

"I'm sorry. I'm not laughing at you exactly. It's that I haven't heard you curse before."

"No Jack, it's just that old man can push my buttons faster than anyone on Gods green earth. I'm sorry I didn't realize I was cursing. Your eyes look funny." Sandy said as she couldn't take her eyes off of Jack's.

"If you think they look funny from where you are you should see them from this side." I said with a laugh. Sandy was laughing so hard that she wiped tears from her eyes.

"How long had it been since she had laughed like that? Too long." She answered her own question. Sandy could tell that from then on it was going to be hard to just keep it a business relationship between her and Jack. Just business she told herself as she went to the stove to fix them dinner.

"I think that I need to lay down." I said as the room started spinning. As I raised from the table I almost blacked out and had to grab the back of my chair to keep from falling.

Sandy ran to Jacks side when she saw him almost fall. "That stuff never effected pa like that. Are you sure your alright? Let me help you." Sandy said as she put my arm around her neck and walked me to my room. Some how we tripped at the bed and Sandy ended up on the bottom. To make matters worse when I tried to push myself off of her, my hand landed on her breast.

Sandy's nipple became erect in the palm of my hand. I may have left my hand on her breast a little longer then it took to push myself off of her. As soon as Sandy was able to get up off the bed she was on her feet. Strictly business. Sandy said as she hurried out the door.

No longer then I had been on top of Sandy, I got an erection. You have to stay away from her. I told myself. I need to stay out of the cities and this is a good place to stay. I closed my eyes and pictured Sandy as I had seen her the night before. Should I risk getting run off from here or getting a sexual relationship with Sandy? As I pictured Sandy in the nude, I made up my mind.

My pa had told me that life was a crap shoot and you never know if you don't roll. I was going to roll and set what came up.

Sandy's heart was pounding like a drum as she left Jacks room. It wasn't that Jack had left his hand on her breast for to long but she could have sworn that he had a hard on while he was there. Sandy believed that if she hadn't left when she had that she would be having sex before dawn. Sandy made her way back to the kitchen, she had a lot of things she had to decide before things went any further. Right now her mind was saying one thing and her body was saying something else. It had only been a day that she new Jack but she felt like she'd known him all her life. He was what her dreams were made of but now he was real and in her life to stay she hoped. She made up her mind right then and there that she would not let this man get away from her. No matter what it took to keep him there.

There was her pa to consider in this too. She had to get Ben to like Jack or about the time she got things lined out. Ben would be sure to come along and mess things up for sure. All this plotting was giving her a headache.

"I sure hope you are worth all this trouble Jack Benson." She said in a whisper. As she thought of seeing Jack in his shorts this morning she decided that he was worth the trouble. The thought made Sandy blush even now. As she lay in bed and talked with her mother she told her mother all about Jack. Her mother approved of Jack, she was also sure. With her ma's approval Sandy dreamed of her life with Jack. The cocks crow woke her up the next morning. Sandy was thankful to the old bird even though it wasn't quit daylight yet.

She was sure that Jack would be laying there in his shorts again. That's why it surprised her that he was already up and dressed when she walked into his room to wake him.

"The old bird really knows his job around here, don't he?" I asked as Sandy came into my room. I sensed a hit of dissapointment in Sandy's voice when she spoke.

"Your up bright and early." She stopped at the door as if she was entering a kingdom of royalty. "You don't have to get up this early Jack. I would be glad to let you sleep until six."

The statement brought a laugh from me. "Should I go back to bed boss?"

"No I'm just saying I'll come and get you up is all."

"Thanks partner! But I think I will pull my load around here." I told her.

"I noticed that you have a tractor out there." I told Ben when he joined us in the kitchen.

"For all the good it's doing me." Ben shot back.

"If you show me where you keep the tools, I'll see what I can do about getting it started!"

"That damn tractor has been there for two years. and I've had a few people tell me it can't be fixed."

"I just thought I would offer." I told Ben as he sat down at the table.

"I'll show you where the tools are." Sandy said. "I dought if the drunken bastard even knows he has any tools! You are going to take me into Greenvilleto stock up on food." She told Ben as she turned to him. "I'll get you some ciggerretts while I'm there." She told me. "You can't handle pa's tobacco, that's for sure."

I had to agree. There was no doubt in my mind who ran this plantation.

After getting a small tool box, I waded through the weeds to where the tractor sat. I took my pocket knife and cleared the weeds from around the tractor so I could work on it. I worked on the old John Deer tractor for about three hours. I was about to decide that those few people Ben had look at this thing just might be right. When they said it couldn't be fixed. I had drained the gas from the tank and bleed the fuel line to the carberator.

I had cleaned the plugs, and looked at all the wires. I was ready to pick up my tools and go back to house when I noticed a break in the ignition wire just under the plastic coating. I cut the wire at the break and spliced it back together. I put my foot on the starter, and the old John Deer lived once again.

I was surprised to see Ben sober as he brought Sandy back from the store. Ben was as surprised to see the old John Deer sitting at the house as he drove in. The look on both their faces told me that they didn't think I could have it running. Ben was speechless as he climbed up on it and hit the starter and she came to life.

"I sure am glad I hired you, Jack." Ben said as he patted me on the back. Sandy knew she wouldn't have to get her pa to like Jack anymore, from the grin on Ben's face he was in love with him too.

Sandy through her arms around my waist and gave me a hug. "I knew you could do it Jack." She said as she squeezed me. I put my arms around her and pulled her braless breast to my chest.

As the three of us sat at the table after we ate Ben told Sandy to put a little extra on my check for fixing the tractor. "I was planning to give him some extra myself." She told Ben with a wink at me.

Something told me that Sandy wasn't talking about money. Ben saw the way they were looking at each other, in a way that brought cold chills to Ben. The way his daughter was looking at Jack, they were more then working partners. What frightened him the most was that when Jack left, he just might take Sandy with him. Ben told himself that he wouldn't let that happen.

If Sandy was to leave him, he would have no one to work the farm. He couldn't allow that. Oh hell. What was he worried about. Jack would get tired of the work and be gone in a few days, and besides there was a lot more stuff for him to fix.

Just the same he was going to keep an eye on them. There was no way he wanted to have a new born baby in this house, no way. "I'm going to bed sissy." Ben told Sandy as he rose from the table.

"Okay pa! I'll wake you in the morning." Sandy told him as she looked at me. I could tell it was for my benefit.

"That's okay sissy! I'll be out on the tractor before you get up." He said as he walked off.

Ben stopped at the door and turned to Jack "I'll get you up at five." Then left the room.

"What in the world are we going to do at five?" I ask Sandy.

"I don't know but it has to do with the tractor." She said as she watched Ben walk away.

The next morning Ben was true to his word and woke me at five. Sandy was already fixing breakfast by the time I reached the kitchen.

"We use to grow hemp here on this place back in nineteen fifty for hemp rope." Ben told me as I sat down at the table. "Well the government makes me mow the hemp down each year and I'm two years behind. This morning we are going to start mowing."

It brought a smile from Ben when I said "Okay your the boss."

It was six o'clock before we reached the field to start mowing. "I'll make the first pass and then you will know where to mow." Ben said over his shoulder as he took off leaving me standing there. Some of the plants were as big as saplings. If it wasn't for the big bud hanging from the limbs you couldn't tell them from the tree's.

I sat on a moss covered rock as I waited for Ben to return. I used the time to think of how I should go about getting Sandy into bed. She sure was pretty enough but it wouldn't be right to start a relationship and some day you will be gone. I will be alright as long as I keep out of public. I told myself. Hell, I'm going to give it a try. I could hear Ben coming back.

Ben had me follow him in the truck so he could leave me there while he went for gas for the tractor or so he said as I climbed on the tractor. I was glad to see him go. I was afraid he was going to stay with me for a while. Now I had all the time I needed to think of a plan that could suit me as well as Sandy. I would have to find out what she was looking for.

Sandy had kept an eye out for any sign of Jack coming back to pack his things. Her heart skipped a beat before she could tell who was driving the truck coming back from the field. She gave a sigh of relief as she saw Ben get out of the truck.

"Sissy, I'm going to get some gas." Ben told her through the screen door.

"You mean your going to get drunk, don't you?" Sandy yelled at him.

"No! No! I'm really going to get gas for the tractor." Ben told her as he went to the truck. Sandy could see two five gallon cans sitting in the back of the truck.

Smiling Sandy thought just maybe he was going for gas. Then she thought of the chance of him getting drunk and not coming back. The smile left her face as she weighed the odds.

Ben hadn't made it to the main road before Sandy had Storm saddled. She reached the field, Jack was no where in sight. From the sound she could tell that he was coming toward her. Storm was moving around like he couldn't stand still so Sandy got off his back and tied him to a tree. She had no sooner got a knot in the reins then she heard the tractor sputter and die. Sandy decided to walk to where the tractor had died.

The tractor had stopped down by the lake and as Sandy reached Jack he had stripped off his clothes and headed for the water. Sandy had thought of yelling and telling Jack that she was there but decided against it. Through Sandy's eye the firm body that lay before then showed a broad shouldered man, well muscled and a round ass. His manhood was nothing to brag about she thought.

Sandy was glad she hadn't announced herself earlier as she watched as Jack would throw his body out of the water like a dolphin. Jacks arms would break the water then he would be out of sight for the longest time. She started getting worried after Jack seemed to have disappeared. She slowly walked to the water's edge and still didn't see Jack. Had he drowned?

Sandy looked the lake over to see if there was movement anywhere. Jack's head broke the water right in front of her. Sandy didn't want to look so surprised but she couldn't help herself. "Are you alright?" She asked as Jack rose from the water without embarrassment. That was alright with Sandy because she was embarrassed enough for both of them. I could tell from the expression on her face that I caught her spying on me.

"I'm sorry Jack! I thought you had drowned."

"You must have been watching me for quit some time." I said with a little laugh so Sandy would know I wasn't mad at her. Sandy turned her back to me while I put my clothes back on.

"You have only been here two weeks and I never worked with a young man before. I have never had to fight with so many feelings these last two weeks." Sandy just kept talking with her back to me. "Pa has done warned not to grow fond of you. He said 'you won't last and that I would get hurt when you left.'"

"Your pa's probably right. But there's a chance that we would love every minute of it."

Sandy turned to face me as she talked. "I know that I'm going to get hurt by you Jack. But I have feelings too." It surprised me when Sandy came right out and told me that she wanted me.

"I can't tell you that I'll be here forever Sandy but I can make it good for the both of us."

"I'm afraid Jack that one morning I would wake up and I would be alone again." Sandy said as she turned her back to me again even though I was fully dressed.

"I'm sorry Sandy but that is how it has to be. There are reasons that I have to do it that way."

Sandy turned and put her arms around me and looked me in the eyes. "I will do it your way Jack. The way I see it I'm either going to get hurt when you leave or hurt all the time you are here. So I'll wait until you leave to hurt."

"I'll try to see to it that you won't be sorry for your decision." I told Sandy Just before I kissed her. Sandy backed up from me and I thought she had changed her mind. "Not here Jack, not like this. I want it to be something that I can keep here with me when you are gone."

It might be thought of as strange but I knew what Sandy was talking about."Do it any way that you want." I told her as I captured her in my arms and kissed her again.

"What about your pa? You know as well as I that he isn't going to just stand there and let us carry on as if we were married." I told Sandy as we both rode Storm back to the house.

"You leave pa to me." Sandy said over her shoulder and kicked Storm in his flanks to speed him up. When I had told Sandy that she could do it her way, I sure didn't know just how far she was willing to take it. Boy did I learn fast.

Ben had always went on a hunt with the boys for a weekend and Sandy was going to have a big surprise when he got back from this one. She told herself. By monday morning she was going to be a married woman. At least Ben would think that she and Jack were married.

When Sandy had told Jack that she was going to get a copy of a marriage certificate and show Ben that they were married. He was just a little bit shy about doing it. Once she had made him understand that it wouldn't be real, did he agree to go along with it.

All three of them were packed in the old truck headed for town. Ben was thinking how good that first bottle of gin was going to be after he had been sober for a week.

"Let me out here!" Sandy told Ben as we drove by the court house. Ben let her out and then parked the truck at a shopping mall.

I went to a pawn shop and got two gold wedding bands for twenty five dollars. The plan was to show Ben the marriage license and let him see the wedding rings. Sandy knew that Ben couldn't read so he couldn't read who was on the paper that Sandy was going to show him.

I really didn't like the idea of lying to Ben but I didn't like the idea of sleeping by myself even less. This plan of Sandy's could work for the both of us. I thought as I walked out of the pawn shop with the two rings in my pocket.

I was to meet Sandy at the restaurant to go over our wedding plans. "Did you get the rings?" Sandy asked as I sat down at her booth.

"Yes I got them. Did you get what you went after?"

"Well, yes and no." Sandy said as she handed me the marriage certificate. "This is a real one. The lady at the court house gave me a real one so all we have to do is sign it."

"That would mean that we were really married!" I told Sandy.

"No it doesn't the lady told me that it was no good if it isn't done by a preacher."

"No one will even know about this except you and me and pa." Sandy said "All this for my pa's benefit Jack not ours." I trusted her so I went along. The weekend for the big hunt finally came.

Sandy knew that it was just an excuse for a bunch of drunks to get drunk together they weren't going to fool her by calling it a hunt. Well when Ben Tall came home this time he was going to see that Sandy Tall was a hunter too. And this time she was bringing her game home with her. A smile stayed on her face all the way home and her eyes were on Jack.

"Did you put htem bottles where they wouldn't get broke sis?" Ben asked Sandy.

"Yes pa! I put them so they won't get broke." Sandy had put the liquor bottles so they wouldn't get damaged. She wanted her pa to drink as many bottles as soon as he could. She wanted him in his bed and passed out early tonight. She had seen Jack's body that day at the lake and had pictured him in her dreams ever since. She had accepted the idea of one day waking up and finding Jack gone. But she knew that before he left she was going to see that he left his seed with her. In her mind she would always have Jack Benson even if it wasn't legal. If her plan worked her pa would think she got pregnant on her honeymoon. From what she had seen of Jack, he had the tools for the job.

Sandy looked at me kinda strange all the way home. From the smile on her face I pretty much knew she was thinking of what we were going to do this weekend. I thought.

"Sandy stop looking at Jack like a rabid dog!" Ben yelled from his side of the truck. "I'm almost afraid to go on this hunt and leave you two alone." Ben said as he looked at me.

"You don't have to worry about that Ben. I'm just a hired hand." I told him.

"It's not you I'm worried about." He said as he moved his eyes to Sandy.

"Oh pa! You know I'm a good girl and I'm waiting for my wedding night." Sandy said with a laugh.

"You see that you do!" Ben said as he returned to driving. I had to turn my head and look away before I burst out laughing. Sandy knew that Ben wasn't going to not go on the big hunt. It was the only place he would be for the next three days.

Sandy had learned about what went on at the big hunt from a girl friend at school. Her pa was like Ben and she knew all about it and told Sandy. Her friend had told Sandy that some of the men had sex with a woman at the same time. Of course Sandy knew better the woman could only have one hole. Sandy tried to picture her pa with a woman and it mad her laugh every time.

She didn't laugh when she thought of her and Jack making love. She sighed. Just as she had finished fixing supper, Sandy went over and opened the cabinet door and told Ben that she put the bottles up there when he wanted it. It worked because as soon as Ben had finished eating he went and got a bottle out and took it to his room.

"Can I see it?" Sandy asked as soon as Ben was out of the room. Jokingly I reached down and started to unzip my pants. "No you silly thing. I mean the ring."

I reached into my pocket and pulled out the two rings. Sandy hastily grabbed the small one and put it on. I reached and stopped her. "I think I'm the one that should put it on, don't you?" Sandy Just shook her head without saying a word. I took the ring and dropped to one knee in front of Sandy. "Will you be my wife?"

"Oh yes!" Sandy said as if she was standing in a church.

"You may kiss the bride!" I said as I rose from kneeling.

"Yes you can!" Sandy managed to get out before my lips covered hers. After that no other words were needed. Passion has it's own language.

Things were going fine until Ben got mine and Sandy's attention by reminding me we were going to start work early. Ben told us as he appeared out of nowhere. He told Sandy to stay because he wanted to talk to her. Sandy's eyes never left me as I walked out of the room. Ben waited till he heard my foot steps on the stairway before he spoke to Sandy.

"Sandra Jean Tall," Pa always used my christian name when he was serious, "I've been watching the way you have been looking at Jack and I don't like it."

"Theres nothing going on between us!" She assured Ben.

"Sissy I may have been born at night but it wasn't last night. If you don't stop acting like a bitch in heat, I'm going to run him off." Fire came to Sandys eyes and Ben knew he had said the wrong thing.

"Pa I love you but if you run Jack off I'm going with him. Do you understand? I told you that there was nothing going on between Jack and me. But if I take the notion to marry Jack I'll do it." Sandy threatened. She didn't realize until she was going to her room that she was still wearing the ring that Jack had put on her finger.

If she's anything like her mother she would marry the boy just for spite. Ben told himself as he stood and watched Sandy turn her back to him and walk out. Sandy had cut out the only option he had of getting rid of Jack. The more Ben thought about it the more he realized that he might be going about this the wrong way. If Sandy could get the boy to marry her he would have a man to work for nothing. Ben decided to have another bottle of gin and think about it somemore.

The night before Sandy had thought of going and getting into Jacks bed just to show her pa but decided against it. Sandy was going to wait until her wedding night, she told herself with a little laugh. By tonight Ben would be gone to the big hunt and her and Jack would have the whole place to themselves.

The justice of the peace would be there at six and Jack still had to be convinced that it was just a ruse. Ben was sitting at the table as Jack walked into the kitchen. Ben's eyes never left Sandy as he watched her reaction as I entered. I thought that Sandy would come to me as soon as she was through with Ben but she didn't. She had told me through the door that we would talk tomorrow. The way Ben was looking at her I could understand why.

I was surprised to see a smile come to Ben's face as his eyes turned to me. "Young man I've got a job for you today."

Sandy's expression didn't change as Ben spoke so I went along at least he wasn't handing me walking papers.

"Okay, what is the job?" I ask as I sat down.

"I've decided to put a fence around those twenty acres we just bush hogged and I need you to dig the post holes. I'll tell you where to get the posts and wire." Ben said as he sipped his coffee.

"Pa you know we don't have enough cattle for that much more land."

"Sissy I think I know what them cows need!" Ben shot back. Sandy knew that if she said any more Ben would know that they had something planned. If she didn't do something Ben was going to ruin her plans.

She was going to feel foolish if the Justice of the Peace came and Jack wasn't there. "One of the cows is giving birth today so I'll need Jack with me."

"Which cow?" Ben asked.

"I don't know, I think it's number three." Sandy said in a mocking voice.

"I didn't know we had a cow to calf."

"Pa you don't even know how many cows we have." Sandy said with confidence. Ben knew he had lost the argument because he didn't know how many cows they did have. I just sat and watched for who won the power struggle. I have to admit that I was relieved when it looked like Sandy won.

"Do what you want." Ben said as he rose from the table. "I'm going to the big hunt and I won't be back until Sunday.

"What's so different from any other week?" Sandy asked as Ben left us at the table.

"Do you mind telling me what's going on." I ask after we was alone. I had to tell him something or he would have ruined our plans.

"You mean we didn't get married last night?" I asked.

"Not exactly." Sandy said. "I was waiting until tonight so we could have the whole place to ourselves." Sandy decided that now was the time to tell Jack about the justice of the peace was coming. "I even called an uncle to come over and pretend he was a preacher."

"Why would we need someone to act like he was a preacher?" I ask. Sandy put her arms around my waist and lightly kissed me.

"The truth is Jack, that I know some day you will pack up and leave and I think that I should at least get a memory out of it." Sandy said as she kissed me again. After taking her lips from my check Sandy reminded me that it wouldn't be legal unless a proper preacher did it.

Sandy's face exploded in a smile as I told her that she had the right to have her memory out of this wedlock. Sandy was so over joyed that her plan had worked so well. Now for part two she said to herself.

I've got to get Jack out of the house so she could get their wedding chambers ready for tonight. "Jack while I'm getting things ready. Why don't you take Jake out for a walk and hall some hay up to the old house."

"I thought that once that Ben was gone we could consummate our marriage." I said with disappointment in my voice. I knew that our wedding was off to a rocky start when Sandy told me that the cows had to eat even if it was our wedding night. "Your the boss." My words cut Sandy to the bone.

"Just in certen things." Sandy said as she grabbed my hand and placed it on her breast.

My eyes never left Sandy's face as I watched for the slightest hint of fear as I moved my hand from her breast and placed it on her mound between her legs. Sandy's mind raced to hide the panic she felt when Jack placed his hand on her.

It's to late to back out now. She told herself as Jack cupped the palm of his hand between her legs. Sandy's emotions were changing so fast that she didn't know which one to grab. She was finally able to hold on to just one as Jack removed his hand from between her legs.

I stepped back and looked at my hand and with a grin. "This kinda makes me the boss." I said and walked out. Sandy didn't know if she should laugh or be angry. what troubled her was that he might just be right.

She spent the rest of the day getting every thing ready for the wedding night for her to remember. She didn't like deceiving Jack but she had made up her mind to have a baby. Jack was going to father the baby.

I didn't like the way things were going. "If I wanted a place to hide then this was the place." I had spoke out loud even though there wasn't anyone around to hear except Jake. "You look like you have done well." As if he had understood me, Jake turned his head as if to say you've got to be kidding.

The gesture brought a smile to my face. The old house came into view. I got off the wagon and Jake went on. As I walked through the old house I could picture the story Sandy had told me. I guess that the aggressive female trait goes back a long way. I thought as I walked through the house.

I'm just glad this make believe marrage between me and Sandy isn't real. I did not care that Sandy told someone besides meabout it. She does know that someday I may not be here and she still wants to play house. I found that I couldn't find a thing wrong with that myself.

As I walked through the field trying to catch up to Jake, I came across a pot plant that stood twenty feet tall. I had a bud as big as my arm hanging in front of me. It was the color of a bright gold as it was moved by the wind. The pungent odor the bud gave off hit my nostrils as I touched the bud. I took out my knife and cut off the golden bud that hung in front of me. By the time I caught up with Jake I had cut off five big buds and was carrying them in my shirt. I put the buds aside until I got the hay off the wagon before I laid them in the back.

The commune I had stayed at for awhile was only two hundred miles away from here. A bud like that would sell for a hundred dollars a piece. I thought as I stared at the five buds I laid back there. Hell that's five weeks of work right there and it hadn't taken five minutes to cut them. This place even came with it's own money tree. I said as I headed back.

Sandy was starting to get worried about Jack because it was going on five o'clock and he hadn't come back yet. Had she pissed him off this morning to where he would just take off? She asked herself. No he would have taken his things and he wouldn't have taken Jake. A sigh of relief exscaped her lips as ahe heard the screen door open. Sandy ran and through her arms around Jacks waist.

"I didn't think you were coming back." She said as she laid her head on my chest. "What is that smell?" She asked as she stepped back from the shirt

I had put back on before coming to the house.

"That my lady is pure gold." I told her.

"Well go wash off that gold dust." Sandy replied as she pointed toward the bathroom. I noticed that Sandy had closed and locked the door to her room. Not thinking anymore about it I went ahead and took my bath.

The Justice of the peace had no sooner pronounced us husband and wife, when Sandy was showing him the door. I was hoping that it was because she wanted to be alone with me. Sandy had put on her mother's wedding dress and her mother must have been the same size when she got married because the dress fit perfectly. She took my hand in hers and led me to her

"What are you doing?" Sandy asked as I put my hand between her legs. Sandy's body shook as if she was having convulsions when Jack took the little bud of her womanhood between his teeth and gently bit it. She got me by the hair on my head and pulled me on top of her. She took my erect penis in her hand and guided me to her.

As I entered her Sandy placed her heels on my ass and started thrusting her hips into me with such force that I thought I might hurt her. The cries she made were from pleasure, not pain. She was pulling me into her so hard that the full length of my penis was out of sight. I hadn't put on a condom so when I felt myself start to explode I tried to pull out.

"No!" Sandy cried as she used her heels to force me back in her. With her heels on my ass I couldn't help but explode inside her.

"Oh baby!" I cried as my body shook from head to toe. I could tell that Sandy had made it by the way she had her eyes closed and her body arched in the air.

Sandy's legs locked around Jack like a vice. I felt like I was in the coils of a big snack. For each move I made to try and get released from her legs, they tightened up more. It was hard to tell who's cries were the loudest mine or Sandy's. I didn't notice the salty sweat in my eyes until I just fell on top of Sandy.

Sandy pulled my head up til we were face to face. "Let's do it again Jack!" She pleaded. How was I going to explain that I needed to take a break between times? I asked myself.

"We will Sandy. I need to go pee first so I'll be ready for the next round." I told her as I went to the bathroom.

If I can have a baby I should do it now. Sandy told herself as she watched Jack. She got Jack to make love to her two more times last night before he fell asleep. She had decided to have two more tries just in case the first one didn't take. Sandy had thought of climbing on Jacks penis this morning when she woke up and saw it but she told herself to let him sleep and get as much rest as he could because she wasn't through with him yet.

Sandy had made breakfast for Jack and had put it on a tray ready to take to him. If he can go three times a night it's not going to take as long to get pregnant as I thought. Sandy told herself as she lifted and headed for her room. Sandy was surprised to see the bed empty as she entered the room. She quickly placed the tray on the foot of the bed and ran to Jacks room. He was standing with his back to her with his bag in his hand.

"Your not leaving ?" She asked before he turned around.

"No." I said as I put Joyces picture back in the bag. "I was getting something to put on after my bath." I told Sandy as I turned around.

"I was afraid you had gone already when I brought you breakfast and you weren't there."

"I'm still here as you can see." I said as I took Sandy in my arms and kissed her. "I can't tell you that I'll be here for good but for now I'm here." As Sandy laid her head against my chest she tried to hear every word he said and how he said it in hopes that he would tell her that he would never leave but he didn't.

"That's alright!" She was going to make him want to stay no matter what, she vowed silently. Sandy took the breakfast tray to the kitchen while Jack took his bath. When Jack made it to the kitchen he saw that Sandy had put his plate at the head of the table.

"Sit and eat your breakfast. It's suppose to be the most important meal of the day. It's where you get all the energy for a day." Sandy said as she pulled the chair out for me. "I want you to get all the energy you can. I didn't know a guy could go three times a night." Sandy said as she sat down.

I started laughing so hard that it brought tears to my eyes. "Baby a man can't go three times every night." I informed her.

"But last night we made love three times didn't we?"

"Yes we did! But I can't do that every night." I told her after I got my laughter under control.

"Your going to need all the energy you can muster." Sandy told me. Not much more was said about sex for the rest of the meal.

Sandy knew that Ben would be back early tomorrow, so she needed to put her time with Jack to good use. "What did you have planned for today?"

"I thought I would go out to that field your pa asked me to fence."

"That can wait for awhile." She said as she raised from the table.

"What did you have in mind?" I asked as I raised also. Sandy let the house coat fall to the floor and stood there naked. "I'm tempted my little rabbit but I've got things to do."

I didn't tell Sandy but I was going to see how many buds I could get into the old house. In a week or so they would be their weight in gold.

"Pa will be back soon Jack. Don't you want to spend time with me?"

"As soon as I get back Sandy we'll make love. I promise." Sandy was disappointed as she picked up her house coat off the floor.

"Wait till I get dressed and I'll go with you." Sandy said as I went out the screen door. By the time I got Jake hooked up to the wagon, Sandy was dressed and there. I tried to think of a way to tell her about the buds that I had already put in the old house. I knew she would find them sooner or later.

"I was thinking about putting a few buds in the old house to dry for Ben!" I told Sandy before we reached the house. "That will be alright won't it?"

"You can do that if you like but pa doesn't smoke that much!" She said as she saw what I had already hung in the old house.

"I know that." I said. "I was just drying different kinds to give him the best ones." Sandy thought it was strange that Jack was going to so much work to please her pa on her wedding day.

When we came out of the house we found that Jake had gone on without us so we walked. "Do you think Ben will believe we are married?"

"As soon as I show him our marriage license."

"But as soon as he reads the names on the license?" I said thinking of the false name I put on it. I had put Jake instead of Jack.

"Pa is iliterate so he can't read a thing." Sandy said. I had to admit that it felt good knowing I was going to be living in sin, as my mom called it, with Sandy. Her long blond hair and blue eyes gave her the look of a model instead of a farm girl. She had proven how little she knew about a man when she thought a man could go three times every night. That one still brought a smile to my face.

We caught up to Jake, he was standing at the lake getting a drink. "Let's get in the water!" Sandy said as she started taking off her clothes. I started to say no until I saw Sandy's nude body as she entered the water.

"Oh! What the hell!" I said and took my clothes off and joined her. As we played in the water we both became excited. The water was up to my chest when Sandy put her arms around my neck and her legs around my waist and lowered herself on me. By the time I got Sandy to shore she was well on her way to orgasm. When I laid down in the grass with Sandy still wrapped around my waist she had already had one. To prevent what had happened last night, I cupped the back of her knees with my arms so she couldn't get me in the vice again. Sandy was at the point where she didn't care how Jack done it just as long as he did.

"Oh yes! Jack right there! I've almost made it. Oh please Jack leave it in."

I think that was the moment I knew what Sandy was doing. My mind was telling me to stop but my body had control at the moment. My mind was losing the battle. I did as Sandy requested and exploded inside her.

"You know don't you?" Sandy asked as I colasped on top of her.

"Yes!" I said as I propped myself up on my elbows to watch her reaction.

"I hope you know I wasn't out to hurt you or stop you from leaving. I just wrapped around my waist she had already had one. To prevent what had happened last night, I cupped the back of her knees with my arms so she couldn't get me in the vice again. Sandy was at the point where she didn't care how Jack done it just as long as he did.

"Oh yes! Jack right there! I've almost made it. Oh please Jack leave it in."

I think that was the moment I knew what Sandy was doing. My mind was telling me to stop but my body had control at the moment. My mind was losing the battle. I did as Sandy requested and exploded inside her.

"You know don't you?" Sandy asked as I colasped on top of her.

"Yes!" I said as I propped myself up on my elbows to watch her reaction.

"I hope you know I wasn't out to hurt you or stop you from leaving. I just their questions. Ain't you Jack?"

As I stood there without answering, Sandy knew I was going and soon. Tears filled her eyes as she watched Jack walk to his room.

Sandy ran into my room as I was putting things back into my bag. "Don't leave Jack! Stay here with me !" Sandy pleaded. "I'll hide you out and no one will ever know Jack. Please!"

"I was telling you the truth when I said I didn't do anything." I told Sandy as I turned around to face her.

"Then why?" Sandy asked holding up her hand to remind me we are partners. I took off my ring and handed it to her.

"The marriage is over." I said and walked out.

"Take me with you." Sandy begged as she followed me out of the house.

"I can't do that. You know how much trouble you would get into if you came with me? No, I told you this day would come and what I was going to do when it did."

Sandy knew that Jack was right. She had known that this day would come. But she had hoped it would take its time. Sandy was crying so hard that she dropped to her knees. With an out stretched hand and one on her stomach. "Say good bye to your pa." She cried as she watched the blur disappear into another tear.

By the time Sandy had gotten the tears wiped from her eyes with the back of her hand, she was on her feet. "I'll never leave you!" She said as she patted her stomach. "I'll always have Jack with me as long as I have you."

Sandy knew that Ben was only trying to protect her, but was in no mood to talk to him. Sandy walked to her room and lay down on her bed and cried herself to sleep. She didn't wake up until five the next morning. Hurried to Jacks room in hopes that it was all just a nightmare.

Bad dream or not. He was gone and she knew he wouldn't be back when she opened the door and everything that Jack owned was gone. Just as she was about to leave Sandy saw the pipe on the night stand. "I'll keep this for you." She said in a low voice as she picked up the pipe and walked out of the room.

By seven o'clock Sandy had Storm saddled and was on her way to the lake. After taking the bridle from Storms mouth so he could graze. Sandy walked to the waters edge. She thought of how, when the law man that came there was looking for a young man alright but his name was Tom Harder not Jack Benson.

Sandy watched as the cool morning air made the white misty cloud rise off the water like a veil. Sandy knew that the water was warmer then the air that caused it. The cool air brought goosebumps to her arms as she striped off her clothes and ran into the water.

Sandy waded into the lake until her head was the only thing sticking out of the water. She closed her eyes and relived the time Jack made love to her. The sound of a branch braking behind her caused Sandy to open her eyes. At first she thought it was Storm behind her. But when she saw Storm, he was a good piece in front of her. She quickly turned to see what had made the noise.

Not seeing anything, Sandy rushed out of the water and quickly dressed Not waiting to put the briddle back in Storms mouth she jumped up in the saddle and rode him home.

I had watched as Sandy had undressed and gotten into the lake from behind some bushes. You don't know how hard it was to just watch her lovely body and not go to her. I had been staying at the old house from the time I had left. I had been stealing food from Ben and Sandy when they were gone. I thought that she had caught me when I got to close and stepped on that branch.

The pot I had drying was about ready to take with me and then I would be gone for good. I wanted to jerk off my clothes and get into the water with Sandy but I knew it would only hurt her more for just a few days of pleasure. I came close to calling out as Sandy rode Storm off in a gallop. I also knew that Ben would turn me over to the law the first time he laid eyes on me. "Maybe if things were different." I said as I watched her go out of sight.

Ben had stayed and helped Sandy for the first week after Jack had left. As soon as he thought that I was going to do the work that he had started staying away again. It had been three weeks since Jack had left and she was late. She knew that it was just two days late but it had given her hope. "What are you going to do if you are Sandy?" She asked herself out loud. Sandy was lifting a bail of hay out of the wagon when she asked herself that.

"If you have a baby, who is going to take care of this place?" She knew better then to think that Ben was going to be any help. Maybe she could hire another young man? Her chances of that was none. After Jack, Ben wasn't about to let that happen. "Don't you worry none J.J. mommy will think of something." Sandy said as she patted her stomach. Sandy had already given her baby a name. Jack Junior.

That night while Sandy sat in front of the mirror she saw the reflection of Jacks pipe laying on her dresser. Sandy remembered seeing a lot of pot that Jack had put in the old house to dry. "I'll go out there in the morning and give it to Ben like Jack had wanted. Sandy thought as she kept brushing her hair. True to her word she rode out to the old house at first light. The room full of pot that once filled the room was gone. All that remained was the string hanging from the walls that Jack had used to dry the pot.

The only thing left there besides the string was the odor. Jack must have taken it with him. She first thought but that couldn't be. She had watched him walk out and he wasn't carrying all that pot when he left. He was there that morning at the lake. It had been Jack that made that noise. Why didn't he say anything? Sandy thought as tears filled her eyes.

Sandy waited until she missed her second period before she went to the doctor so he could confirm that she was pregnant.

"Your two months pregnant and we can't tell what sex it is yet." the doctor said.

"J.J. is going to be a boy!" Sandy said as she took her feet out of the stirrups and stood up.

"Young mothers have a way of knowing those things." The doctor saidwith a laugh.

"Yes we do!" Sandy said as she dressed. What was she going to tell Ben. He was sure to ask what the doctor said when he saw her. Ben was sitting in the truck out in the parking lot when Sandy came out. Sandy had to move an empty bottle from the seat before she could sit down.

"Are we ready to go home now?" Ben asked as Sandy closed the truck door.

"Yes pa! We can go home so you can lay down."

"I was wanting to go home so you could lay down." Ben said in a sober voice. "A young girl that's going to have a baby needs all the rest she can get." Ben said as he drove from the parking lot.

"How did you know?" Sandy asked surprised.

"Sissy I may be old but I'm not dumb. Its been almost three months ago that boy was staying with us and no matter what we do nature will take its course. I've had to do a lot of thinking in the last few months and I didn't like what I thought. There's no way you can work the farm if you have a baby. I can't hire someone else like that boy. So I'm going to do it myself so my grand baby will have a place to live until he grows up. Then I can go to my grave knowing that this farm is still in Tall hands."

If I knew pa would change so much, I would have gotten pregnant sooner. Sandy thought.

Ben ended up hiring a man to work for them. A forty year old black man.

Ben said he gave the place spirit. Sandy didn't mind having John work because he was a good worker. With a black hair and blue eyed boy wanting to put her tit in his mouth all the time, Sandy had to give all her time to JJ.

Sandy brushed the black curls on JJ's head as he wrapped his tongue around her nipple and sucked with all his might. "You sure are going to be just like your daddy." Sandy said with a smile when she pulled her breast from JJ's mouth and he started crying. Sandy patted him on the back til he burped.

Once he had done that he went right to sleep. As Sandy lay JJ in his bed that Ben had dug out of the storage building and put in her room. Sandy couldn't get over how Ben was just so proud of JJ, as if he was Ben's son. He still drank but only on the weekends.

JJ was turning twenty and some if his biker buddies was giving him a cook out party. He was going to get drunk and stoned til nothing else mattered. If it hadn't been for his grandpa and a black man named John, he wouldn't know how to act like a man.

His mom raised him from the age of ten by herself or who ever she was living with at the time. He had gotten so tired of hearing how much he looked like his father from his mother. From what JJ could get out of the story, he was the product of a man on the run from the law. JJ decided he wouldn't waste his time on Jack Benson, the hit and run bastard didn't deserve the time in his mind. Besides he had a party to go to and he wasn't going to let the bastard ruin it for him.

As JJ combed his black hair, he had those big blue eyes starring back at him. He was grateful to the old bastard for one thing, if JJ did look like him. He was a pussy magnet. It seemed that JJ had the pick of the litter, so to speak.

Like tonight he was going by the Well's place and pick up their daughter. Brandy Well's a beautiful blond with green eyes and shaped like a brick out house. Her father is the county judge and a very rich man. Brandy would sneak out of the house after her mother and father went to sleep, that was usually around nine o'clock. She would watch for JJ's headlight and meet him down by the highway.

As long as I got her home before five we were pretty much safe. JJ smiled as he remembered about two weeks ago. It was almost six before he got Brandy home. But as his luck would have it, she was able to get into bed and under the covers before her mother came to wake her.

JJ liked Brandy but he was to free spirited to just go with one girl. Hell he took the conquest of the woman race his personal job. The list of the ones he had already conquered was quite long now. He picked up his sunglasses as he walked out to his 39 Indian. JJ slung his leg over the bike and shoved the kick starter down in one motion. The bike started like a new one. JJ did all the work on his own bike. He didn't trust anyone else to touch it.

"Your the only woman that can give me a thrill every time we go out." JJ said as he patted the gas tank on it's side at sixty miles an hour. Most of the people that was coming to the cook out was already out at the old house keeping the fire going in the Bar-B-Q.

JJ cut his engine and coasted up to Brandy's driveway. He didn't have to wait long before Brandy appeared from the darkness. She got on the bike behind him.

"Hang on tight!" JJ said as he kicked the starter and took off through the darkness. Brandy laid her head on his back and put her arms around him. Brandy was holding on so tight that JJ could tell she was bra less.

By using a back road just big enough for his bike. JJ was back at the party in just a few minutes. As JJ and Brandy got off the bike, a very drunk Buck Well's came up to JJ carrying a glass of beer and in the other hand he was packing a joint that had long since gone out. Buck was no kin to Brandy, they just had the same last name.

"Here you need to catch up with the rest of us!" Buck said as he handed JJ the joint.

"Sure Buck! As soon as we get a beer to wash it down with." I said as I kept on walking. After getting some beer from the keg, JJ went and watched the washer game that was being played by the fire.

"Here hit this JJ !" Buck insisted as he came up to where Brandy and JJ were standing.

The only reason JJ invited Buck was that he was the only one who knew how to cook deer in the ground. JJ knew that the best way to get rid of Buck was to hit the joint. JJ took the joint from Bucks hand and lit it up.

As soon as the sent if the joint hit Jack's nose he knew it was the skunk weed he had sold to someone else. It had one drawback and that was it left you smelling like a skunk. after you smoke the stuff you got used to the smell but a person that didn't smoke could smell nothing but skunk.

"This is some good shit!" Buck said in a slurred voice.

"Dam the luck. Now I'm going to smell like a skunk all night. Brandy doesn't want to smell me like this!" Jj said in a raised voice. JJ almost felt sorry for Buck when he told JJ that he was just trying to get him high and went to the next man down the line.

I didn't realize until Brandy took her hand in mine and took the joint from my fingers. "You'll smell!" I said as Brandy started to hit it.

"If I'm close to you all night." She said with a smile. "I'm going to smell like you anyway." Brandy said as she took a hit. The only part I caught was the all night part.

"Has my brother been bothering you?" Bunny asked as her boyfriend Mark walked up to JJ and Brandy.

"No! He was just giving us a joint." Brandy said as she handed Bunny the joint.

"I se you found the beer wagon." Mark said as he approached JJ.

"It wasn't hard to find after you left mark." JJ said with a laugh.

"Do like my beer" Mark said in a voice that told JJ that he hadn't taken offence. Bunny on the other hand was envious of Brandy because she had eyes for JJ too.

"What is the judges daughter doing at a totally illegal party?" Bunny asked.

"I assure you that I'm not wearing a wire." Brandy said as she pulled up her shirt and exposed her bare breast to everyone. JJ and Mark thought it was funny but Bunny didn't think it was.

"What's so damn funny?" Bunny asked as she hit Mark on the arm. You could tell that Bunny was in the habit of doing it by the way Mark tightened his arm just before she hit him.

"Let's go!" Brandy said as she grabbed JJ by the arm and headed for a different group of people. Bunny was giving Mark hell, JJ saw as he looked back.

"That stuff is selling like hot cakes." Tony said as JJ and Brandy walked by.

"That's good!" JJ said as he kept walking with Brandy in front of him. JJ stopped when Tony reached out and grabbed Brandy by the arm. "If you want to get anymore of that weed you best take your hands off my girl." JJ said as he reached and jerked Tony's hand off of Brandy's arm.

"Sorry JJ! I didn't mean to piss you off." Tony said as he took a step back to let JJ and Brandy go by.

"I need to talk to you." Dan said as him and Gary walked up behind him. JJ turned around and Dan saw who he was with.

"Okay!" JJ said as him and Brandy stopped.

"Can we talk in front of her?" Dan asked.

"If you can trust me then she can hear every word you say."

"Alright here it is. Gary and I met this man who wants five hundred pounds of weed." The amount that the man wanted surprised JJ.

"Where did you meet this man?"

"We met him at a party last week." Gary said.

"No!" JJ said as he shook his head. "I don't like it. This smells like a set up."

"No! No! He ain't no law man. I'm sure." Dan said as he tried to get JJ to go through with the deal.

"You can't tell that about someone you did not know two weeks ago."

"He'll never see you JJ. All you got to do is front us the pot." Dan said.

"I'll have to think it over Dan. Then I'll let you know."

"It's up to you!" Dan said. "But we could make a lot of money if you will go along."

"I'll think it over like I said." Dan knew not to push to hard or JJ wouldn't sell him a joint if he made him mad. The most JJ had ever sold was fifty pounds. He was as nervous as a long tailed cat in a room full of rocking chairs.

It was a simple delivery and pick up the cash but JJ thought for sure that every car he saw was an under cover cop. JJ decided that tonight Brandy was the only thing he was going to think about, everything else could wait. Brandy felt good that JJ trusted her enough that he went about his regular business with her there.

She had been raised by her father, the judge, to be on the side of the law. In most cases she was like that, but wasn't hurting anybody. He was just giving them what they wanted and making a lot of money doing it. She didn't care to much for the story that JJ's real dad was a man on the run for the murder of two teenagers. JJ's mom didn't seem to believe the story and she would know. Brandy was also told that JJ looked just like his dad. If he does she could understand Sandy's love for him.

JJ could make the rest of the world disappear while they were making love. The sounds the smells of lust would take over your mind and you become a wild animal with a hunger that can not be quenched.

Brandy's face saddened as she thought of how the other girls must have felt about JJ before she got with him. She knew that she wasn't the only girl in JJ's life but as often as she and JJ were together. He didn't have time for too many girls besides her.

"Something wrong?" JJ asked as he hooked Brandy in his arms and stared at her with those bright blue eyes.

"No baby! I was just thinking of how much I love you." Brandy said. She had no sooner got the words out of her mouth, then she realized that she had just said the word love. JJ Tall din't believe in love just lust. He unhooked his arm from around her and dropped to his side.

Brandy saw a smile come to Bunnies face as JJ took his arm from around her. She must have been following them like a vulture following a dying man. She thought. "I'm sorry JJ I was not thinking when I said that. I know how much you hate the word love."

"Its not that I don't believe in love. Its just that most people that say that, can't be trusted." JJ said. As JJ saw the grin on Bunnies face he smiled and hooked his arm back around Brandy. "I know a spot just the other side of the lake." He lead Brandy off into the darkness.

"I see from your file that that you been at this for a long time, Mr. Benson." Judge Wells said as he looked at the dark haired man sitting across from him.

"I've done this for for fifteen years, Judge!" Jack said.

"We know that there is someone around here selling huge amounts of pot. We had an undercover agent get close to finding out. But whoever it is he smelled a rat and didn't show up."

"I've worked for the DEA for fifteen years and I made an arrest in every case I've worked." Jack said. "If you don't mind Judge, I just got to town. There is someone I need to look up. So I will wait till tomorrow to start this case." Jack replied as he rose from his seat.

"Sure Mr. Benson. This can wait for another day if you like."

"By the way Judge Wells, do you know if a Sandy Tall still lives around here."

"Yes her and her boy still live out at the old plantation."

Jack had not thought of Sandy being married and with children. Jack fought with emotions of going to see Sandy and not letting her know if he was still alive. The Judge hadn't said anything about a husband. Jack thought as he turned between two old rotten wagon wheels that lead to Sandy's house.

What was he going to say to her when he did see her? He asked himself as he got out and closed the door to his car. Jack stood and waited until someone came to the door even though the screen door wasn't locked. Jack noticed that the place was being took care of real good. He noticed how the out buildings and the house had recently been painted.

"Can I help you?" A voice said from the other side of the screen. Sandy's heart dropped to her knees when she opened the door enough to see who stood out side. If it hadn't of been a few wrinkles Sandy would look just like the first time Jack saw her. "Jack is that you?" Sandy asked as she through her arms around him.

Jack started to tell her that she looked as good as the first time he saw her, when his words were cut off by Sandy's lips on his.

"Come in." Sandy said as she pulled Jack into the house. "Where have you been? How long are you here for?" Sandy asked not giving Jack the time to answer before she asked a different question.

"I'm in town on business." Jack told her just to stop the questions.

"Stay here!" Sandy insisted.

"No! That won't be right to ask your husband to let me do that." Jack said.

"I don't have a husband." Sandy said with a laugh.

"I'm sorry! I was told that you have a son." Jack said in a surprised voice.

"You don't know do you?"

"Know what?"

"JJ stands for Jack Junior. JJ is your son Jack, not just mine." Blood drained from Jack's face as he learned that he was a father of a twenty year old boy. "Are you alright?" Sandy asked as she ran to Jack's side. "You look sick."

Once Jack got back his composure he asked Sandy. "Where is the boy?"

"He's probably out with that girl of his. It's a different girl each week. I quit counting. Oh Jack! He's just like you were all them years ago. A wild stallion on one end and a puppy on the other. He even gets mad when I tell him I love him." Sandy said as the smile left her face.

"What do you do?" Jack asked.

"I told him I was his mother and I was going to love him if he liked it or not." Jack could see that the last twenty years hadn't cooled the fire in Sandy.

"I'll be sure and not tell him that I love him when I see him." Jack said with a little laugh.

"When you see how much the two of you look alike. You will think you turned the clock back twenty years." Sandy said. "So you will stay here?"

"No I have a room in town and my work pays for it." Jack said.

"What kind of work do you do"

"I'm a sales rep. for a big company."

"I'm sure they won't mind you staying here with me." Sandy said as tears formed in her eyes. The sound of JJ's bike brought Sandy and Jacks attention to the outside.

Sandy wiped the tears from her eyes and put a smile in its place. "JJ this is your father Jack Benson." Sandy said as soon as JJ came through the door.

Sandy didn't have to tell JJ who the dark haired man was standing with his hand stretched out to shake his hand. If JJ ever wanted to know what he would look like in twenty years all he had to do was look at Jack. Jack put his arm down when JJ made no move to shake his hand.

"Jack Junior shake your fathers hand." Sandy gave an order, not a question.

"No, the boy is right! I didn't know he even existed until an hour ago." That statement shocked JJ because up til then, he had thought that Jack knew about him but didn't care. "I should be going." Jack said as he started toward the door.

There was so many questions JJ wanted to ask this man. If he let him go, he may never get the chance. "Please stay Jack?!" A smile stayed on Jack's face as he went and sat back down.

It was dark by the time Jack got back to his room to go over the police reports of who the known dealer's were around. The list seemed to have no end. Jack took a red pin and marked under the name he was going to check out starting tomorrow.

Maybe I should have stayed with Sandy. Jack thought. The trouble with that was that it might put Sandy and JJ's lives in danger. No he would keep them out of his life until this case was closed.

The memory of Sandy in the lake that morning almost made Jack change his mind. He did fall asleep with Sandy, in the misty lake, on his mind and a smile on his face. At five in the morning Jack awoke in a cold sweat, hearing the prison doors slam behind him over and over. Jack had served five years before the DEA got him out to work under cover for them.

Jack went ahead and took a shower. Then started reading the other agents report about trying to buy five hundred pounds from a Gary and Dan. Jack just shook his head and said "The dumb bastard tried for to much. The way Jack planned to do it was spend a lot of money around town and have Mr. Big come find him. Jack left the hotel and drove to the only restraurant in town to eat breakfast.

There were several people in there, but three men sitting in the next booth. Jack recognized from descriptions that he had read in the reports as : Dan Buckles, Gary and Tony Mays. Jacks head was pointed away from the three men. He could hear every word they were saying. And they couldn't see Jacks face.

It still surprised Jack just how much he could from loose talk. The three were talking like they were the only people in the place. Jack couldn't believe his luck. From the looks of the three they had been out all night doing something.

"We need to sell some pot and make some money." Dan said as he sipped his coffee.

"That damn bastard JJ! Won't sell me a joint anymore." Tony said in a drunken slur.

"We had a chance to make a bunch of money!" Gary said. "If JJ had just went along with us."

Dan came to JJ's defense. "JJ knows what he is doing." Jack felt sick when he heard JJ's name.

This town was to small for there to be more then one JJ in it. At first when the sheriffs deputy came in and started walking toward Jack's booth. Jack thought he might blow his cover before he got started. There was not suppose to be anyone know about him, except the Judge.

"Your a stranger around here? What's your business here?" He asked as he approaches Jacks table.

"Just passing through." Jack said as he rose from the table. "Do you have a reason for all these questions?"

"We run a tight ship around here." The Deputy said. "I'm going to be keeping my eye on you." And walked off. Jack saw the way the three were watching his every move. So he gave the Deputy a finger behind his back. Which brought laughter from all three.

"The law dogs are pretty bad around here, ain't they?." Jack asked as he threw a twenty dollar bill on the table and left.

Tony moved to the booth Jack had just left and picked up the twenty.

"What are you doing?" Dan asked from the other booth.

"I'm going to buy that mans five dollar breakfast." And put the money in his pocket.

"Who was that?" Gary asked.

"I have no idea! But he don't like law dogs. So he can't be all bad."

As Jack drove to Sandy's house, he thought of how he found out he has a son just in time to arrest him. Of course he didn't know that JJ was Mr. Big yet. It wasn't hard to see that he might be.

Sandy was so glad to see Jacks car drive up that she ran out the door, letting the screen slam shut behind her. Sandy was glad that JJ was up and gone already. Had left her with an empty house for her and Jack.

She had thought all night of the time her and Jack had made love by the lake and made JJ. Back then she had made love to Jack in hopes of having a baby. This time she wanted Jack just for the sex.

She didn't understand why Jack didn't stay with her but she was glad to be with him even if it was just for a little while. Jack had no sooner got out of the car then Sandy was in his arms. Sandy thought it funny that the first thing Jack asked was "Where's JJ?"

"Oh he's gone for the day." Sandy said as she pressed her breast into Jacks chest. She almost made Jack forget why he was there for a minute. "We have the whole house to ourselves." She lead Jack into the house.

Jack couldn't decide if he should tell Sandy that he was a DEA agent or keep quiet and find out as much about his sons work habits. He decided to keep the fact that he was a DEA agent to himself for now.

Once inside the house Sandy just kept pulling Jack toward the bedroom. As soon as Jack saw the bed, he knew what he was in for and he wasn't going to fight it.

"Make love to me Jack!" Sandy said as she pushed him onto the bed. Before Jack could say yes or no Sandy was on top of him with her lips pressing hard on Jacks lips. Passion blanked out everything on Jacks mind to where all he was thinking of was making love to Sandy. Her movements were so slow that she could hardly be seen moving.

"Is something wrong?" Jack asked as he watched her.

"NO, there's nothing wrong! Its just that I've been dreaming of this moment for so long that I want to make it last as long as I can." Sandy said as she kissed me again. She got off the bed just long enough to strip off her clothes. Jack was unbuttoning his shirt when Sandy grabbed his hand to stop him.

"Let me!" She said as she gently laid Jacks hand down by his side. Then took over what he had started. As Sandy undid Jacks belt and snap on Jacks blue jeans, his erect penis pushed its way to freedom except for his briefs.

Sandy rose from the bed to take off Jacks shoes and jeans. As she looked at Jack laying there in his briefs she thought of the time she had seen him like that. Sandy dragged her breast over Jacks stomach and chest as she crawled up between his legs to kiss him.

Sandy took the tip of her tongue and flicked Jacks nipple as she slowly lowered her head lower on Jacks body. She hooked her fingers in the waistband of his briefs and pulled them off of a fully erect penis.

"You don't have to." Jack said as he watched what Sandy was about to do. The only sound that came from Sandy was "Shh." Sandy lowered her head until her open mouth took in as much of Jack as she could take for the first time. Jack wasn't a fan of feleto at all it had to do with the womans teeth being so close to to such a delicate tool.

So far Sandy had kept her teeth well off of his tool but Jack was afraid of it being her first time, she might be dangerous. When Sandy did start using her teeth she was gentle with them. Jack could feel himself build up pressure so he grabbed Sandy's head to stop her.

As gentle as he could, Jack pulled Sandy up to his side and once she was there, got between her open legs. Jack extended one of Sandy's legs until it was pointed toward the ceiling. As he took her foot and ankle in his hand he started making a trail with his tongue down her entire thigh while massaging her foot. By the time Jacks tongue made it to the junction of Sandy's legs he started on the other leg. The warm wet tip of his tongue had no sooner touched the tiny bud of her womanhood then it sent her body into convulsions. Before Jack saw it coming Sandy had gotten him by the hair of the head and was pulling his body like he weighed nothing.

"Now! Jack now! Oh please! Now Jack!" Sandy begged as she pulled him. Passion was so thick you could smell it in the air. The sound of JJ's bike caused Jack to stop but Sandy wrapped her legs around Jack and her eyes pleaded for him to finish.

As JJ and Brandy entered the kitchen, Jack and Sandy came out of her room.

"Mom, what have you been doing with him?" JJ asked as Jack and Sandy approached them.

"You ain't as smart as I give you credit for JJ. If you don't know." Sandy said as she walked past him toward the kitchen to make some coffee.

Brandy turned red as a beet but let out a laugh she couldn't hide. JJ didn't think it was funny at all. To him this man was a stranger even if he was his father. Jack recognized Brandy from a picture of her in his den where they talked. She had never seen him but he was going to be careful of what he says around her.

This was turning into the strangest case he had ever worked on in his fifteen years on the job. It was going like this… He was hired by the Judge Wells to bust a pot ring. Now he learns he has a twenty year old son who is dating the Judges daughter. And his son is the prime suspect for the pot ring.

Jack decided right then that he had enough of DEA work, and as soon as this case was closed he was going to retire.

"Would you like to have a cup of coffee and talk son?" Jack asked.

"Yes I would like to chat with you. While you explain how you was on the run for the murders of two teenagers!" JJ said in a smart tone. The anger that was in JJ's voice and to be talking to his father like that even surprised Brandy. Jack had had about enough of this little upstart in front of him.

"Yes! I'll tell you anything you want to know." Jack said as he got JJ by the shoulder and walked him to the kitchen table. Jack pulled a chair out and sat JJ down in it. "Sit!"

Sandy was in shock as to what was going on. "What's going on here?" She asked Brandy as she stood beside her.

"I think JJ just got his first whopen." Brandy said.

"To set you straight about those two teenagers you think I murdered. They were friends of mine and over the age 21. They took drugs that a man just made and they died. The only thing I'm guilty of is knowing them and being a good friend. If your talking about my five years in prison, that was because I took some pot from this place and tried to sell it to an undercover cop. I spent my time for my crime just like you will if your doing the same thing I did." Jack said before he could stop himself.

"What are you saying Jack?" Sandy asked. "Is JJ wanted by the law? Is that what your saying?" Sandy turned her attention to JJ. "Is what Jack is saying true? Are you selling pot from here?"

JJ said. "No Mom!" But she could tell when he was lieing, always could.

"How about it Brandy?" Jack asked as he turned his eyes on her. "Have you seen JJ sell pot to his friends?"

"You keep her out of this!" JJ shouted.

"That's what you should have done." Jack said.

"Your a law dog!" JJ replied.

"I'm nobodies dog, boy. I do not bow to any man or drug. Yes I work for the DEA and they sent me here to find you."

"You don't have anything on me!" LL said in his own defense.

"JJ, I'm telling you this because I have been there and believe me you don't want to go down that path."

"They'll never prove a thing on me." JJ insisted. "I'll never tell them anything."

"You may not JJ, but you can't say that about everyone you have sold to. Can you?" Jack asked. "What about her?" Jack said pointing to Brandy.

"When they get her in court they will have a different Judge do her case and he won't go easy on her." Brandy became frightened after hearing what Jack was saying. Up until now she had never thought of going in front of a different Judge.

"Jack you've got to do something!" Sandy cried. "You can't send our son to prison! You just can't!" JJ watched Jack to see what his next words would be.

"No! If he quits selling, and I mean to anyone, I'll say that ever who it was got away."

"He agree's!" Sandy said for JJ.

"This is on your shoulders JJ. You are the only one that can stop it from happening." Jack said.

"What about me?" Brandy asked. with the look of a fresh whopped puppy.

"As long as you help keep my son on the straight and narrow. I'll forget to tell the Judge you were involved."

"And what about us?" Sandy asked as she sat down in Jacks lap.

"Well I know a man who is about to retire and is looking for a ready made family."

"Wait here!" Sandy said as she jumped up from his lap and ran to her room. She was back in a flash with two gold bands in her hand.

"No I can't." Jack said as he handed the rings back to Sandy. Sandy's heart dropped from her chest when Jack said he was already married. "I told myself that when this case was closed that I was going to quit and live with her out in the country." Jack said as he reached into his pocket and pulled out a one carrot diamond ring and placed it on Sandy's hand.

"Mrs. Jack Benson will you marry this retired law dog?" Jack asked then looked at JJ. "And this time for real."

"Oh yes Jack! I have been your wife for twenty years and another fifty sounds good to me!" Sandy hadn't gotten the words out of her mouth before her lips were covered by Jacks.

"It looks like you have a father now!" Brandy said as she took hold of JJ's hand.

"He may be the next man screwing my mom but he will never be a father to me." JJ said as he let go of Brandy's hand and walked off.

Brandy felt funny standing there by herself while Jack and Sandy kissed.

"What do you think of this JJ?" Sandy asked before she saw that Brandy was standing there all alone. "Where's JJ?" A smile left her face.

Brandy didn't say anything she just pointed in the direction JJ had gone. Sandy started to go after him when Jack put out his hand and stopped her. "Let him get use to it in his own time."

Sandy's eyes turned from Jack to the direction JJ had gone. "I hope your right." She said with the first words of doubt, Jack had ever heard come from her.

Her love for JJ and Jack was beyond question and she remembered how good Jack was at work back in his younger days. Yet she had never seen him around kids before. I hope being a father is like the mother instincts. Sandy thought.

"I'm going to see the Judge, would you like a ride home?" Jack asked as he turned to Brandy. She looked at the empty hallway were JJ had left her.

"Yes, that would be good." Brandy said as she headed for the door. As Jack got in and closed his door Brandy asked him to let her out before they got to her house.

"Your dad doesn't know about you and JJ?"

"Well no, he doesn't. And I'd like to keep it that way. You see, he doesn't know how much I love JJ."

"From the way JJ treats you I would say that your love only goes one way." Jack said as he put the car in gear and drove off.

"This will be alright." Brandy said as they came in view of her driveway. "You remember what you promised." She said as she got out of the car and closed the door.

"I'll keep mine as long as you keep yours." Jack said as he drove off.

"I think it was just someone passing through Judge." Jack said as he sat in Judge Wells den.

"Could be but the other agents seem to think he is local." The Judge said as he lit a cigar.

"I'll keep looking but I'm not getting much from the people on that list I was sent." Jack said as he rose from his chair.

"You keep trying Mr. Benson. I'm sure you will find out more. After all you have only been here a few days. I don't expect you to pull a rabit out of a hat."

"Well thank you Judge Wells. I will do my best to find whoever is involved and bring them in no matter where they run too." Jack said as he walked out.

Brandy was at the top of the stairs when Jack and her dad walked out of the den.

"Oh sweetheart, this is Mr. Benson. Mr. Benson this is my daughter Brandy."

"How do you do?" Jack said. "Nice to meet you Brandy."

"She is going to take over my practice someday." The judge said.

"If I find out anything at all I'll be sure and come by to tell you." Jack said as his eyes were on Brandy.

"Nice meeting you Mr. Benson." Brandy said as Jack was walking off. As Brandy started to go to her room the Judge asked her to step into his den, that he had a question or two. With every step down the stairs Brandy heart sunk.

"I didn't want to say anything to you around Mr. Benson but I have learned from a good source that you have been seen with that JJ Tall."

"Yes daddy! I have been seeing JJ Tall for a few weeks now. We are just good friends."

good friends."

"Girl you won't get to be a lawyer if hang out with the likes of him. That boy is just like his father, bound for prison. If you don't stop seeing him, you will need a lawyer instead of becoming one."

"I know what I'm doing daddy! I am eighteen years old and I will see whom ever I want." Brandy said as she turned and went to her room.

"You stay away from.." The judge said as he heard Brandy slam her door shut. "Maybe I can get Mr. Benson to help me get rid of that JJ Tall." The Judge said as he walked back into his den.

The sun was setting low when Jack pulled his car up to the restaurant and went in and sat down. A very drunk Tony was more or less laying in his favorite booth. Jack went to the trunk of his car and got out a bag of pot and put it in his pocket. Jack let the bag fall out as he passed Tony's booth and quickly picked it up before anyone but Tony could see it.

Tony was grinning from ear to ear as he asked Jack to sit down. Jack looked the room over before he accepted. "Is that some good shit?" Tony asked.

"I don't know." Jack said. "You see the man I paid to test it for me didn't show up and after I gave him a hundred dollars to test it for me."

"What do you mean test it?" Tony asked.

"I mean smoke it and tell me if its any good." Jack said as he constantly scanned the room as he talked.

"You mean you pay someone to smoke your pot for you?" Tony asked still not believing what he was hearing.

"That's right. I have a lung condition that won't let me smoke anymore. I have to know how good the pot is before I buy a bunch of it."

"Is that job open now that the other man didn't show?"

"Well I don't know." Jack said. "The other man I know I can trust and I don't even know you. You may be a cop or something."

"Could you talk a little louder?" Tony asked as he pulled his shirt as if there was a mic in it. Jack let out a laugh that echoed through the room. everyone seemed to be looking at them.

"This place is making me nervouse." Jack said. "I don't think my man is going to show up."

"We can go to my trailer." Tony said as he stood up with Jack.

On their way to Tony's trailer Jack explained how he put up the money for some big drug deals and paid the people that work with him.

"Well, I'll test the weed for you and only charge you fifty dollars." Tony said with a laugh. He couldn't believe his drunk luck as he sat at the coffee table and rolled a joint from the bag that Jack gave him.

Dan and Gary wasn't going to believe that he was getting paid to smoke another mans pot. "The best way to test this is to roll a small joint and see what a little bit will do for you."

"You probably know more about that then I do." Jack said like he was taking in every word Tony said.

"It has a good smell." Tony said after he lit it up. Jack didn't have to wait long for Tony to fall asleep after he gave him pot treated with a knock out drug. After going through Tony's things Jack picked up the bag of pot and left.

Tony was right! When Dan and Gary heard about what had happened to him, they didn't believe him. Jack had left a hundred dollars on the table where the pot had been. The three of them decided to look up JJ and get some pot with it.

"Hey that's the mans car sitting there." Tony said pointing toward Jacks car. "Damn I hope JJ don't take my job away."

JJ came out to meet them before they got to the house. "You got any pot for sale?" Dan asked as JJ reached them.

"No! I don't sell pot anymore." JJ said.

"Your joking right! Your pulling our leg."

"No! I'm serious. I can't be doing that with my old man here." JJ said pointing toward Jacks car.

"That man is your dad?" Tony asked with a smile.

"Yes." Was all JJ said.

"Hell buddy! He's got better pot then you do. I would say. I smoked some he had and it put my lights out for hours."

JJ thought at first of telling Tony that they should stay away from Jack. Then decided to let them find out on their own. After hearing what happened to Tony JJ was sure Jack was going to set Tony up for the bust.

"How about it JJ? Are you going to sell me some pot or what?" Tony asked.

"I don't have anymore. I got rid of all I had yesterday." JJ said

"Well go ask your pa if he'll sell us some." Tony said eagerly. Before JJ could answer him Jack came out the door. When Jack saw the four of them talking he decided to go see how much damage had been done.

"Tell him Mr. Tall that its alright to sell us some pot like you have."

"I didn't buy that batch of pot and JJ doesn't sell anymore. If you want to deal with me then okay. But if not then stay away. I'll let you know when I get some." Jack told them.

JJ gave Jack a hard look but didn't say anything until the three had left. "Are you going to bust my friends?"

"Not if I don't have to." Jack said "Look JJ I have never let a dealer off the hook before you so don't expect me to let everyone that knows you off too."

"They are just small fish in a big pond." JJ said trying to change Jacks mind.

"A piranha is a small fish with big teeth." Jack said as he went in the back door.

"What was that all about?" Sandy asked as Jack came through the door.

"Me and JJ were just trading fish stories."

"I'm glad you two are talking sports." Sandy said. Jack smiled as he pulled Sandy to him to kiss her.

JJ was mad at Jack for setting up his friends but he was more mad at himself for wanting to cover his own ass first. One thing JJ knew and that was that somebody was going down and it wasn't going to be him. A smile came to JJ's face as he thought of the man that wanted five hundred pounds that Dan had told him about.

A worried look came to Jacks face as he heard JJ's motorcycle started up and leave.

"Something wrong?" Sandy asked.

"No. I was just thinking of something I need to do before tomorrow." Jack said as he kissed Sandy goodbye.

"Maybe I should have started smoking pot back then." Sandy said. It seems that Jack and JJ both were always on the go. So it must work like speed. She thought. Sandy looked at the diamond ring Jack had put on her finger as she watched him drive away. If it came down to JJ or Jack, who would she choose? Don't be silly Sandra you know who.

Jack could see JJ's bike in front of Tony's trailer by the porch light that Tony kept on. Jack had to laugh as he noticed that around the rest of the trailer was completely dark. Jack parked the car and just walked up behind the trailer in the dark and down in the weeds not more then ten feet from them.

"I don't know if we can get a hold of the man again." Dan was saying as Jack sat down. "If we can get a hold of him can we get the pot from you?" Tony asked as he licked the paper on a joint.

Jacks heart sank as JJ said yes. What man can they be talking about? Jack almost laughed out loud when the answer came to him. Jack did burst out laughing after he got back to his car. He knew he should of stayed and learned more but he was afraid they would say something and he'd get caught.

Jack was at the Judges house early the next morning. "I want you to put that agent back on the street and tell him to let it be known that he wants to buy three hundred pounds."

"Do you have a suspect?" The Judge asked. Before Jack could answer, the judge brought up JJ's name.

"No! Young Mr. Tall is not a suspect at this time."

"Well if his name comes up I want to know about it." The judge said as he studied Jacks reaction.

"Let me get these suspects cleared up first then we will look at Mr. Tall."

"I don't want to get the boy in any trouble or anything but I get this feeling that he's in there somewhere." The judge said as he lit a cigar.

"As long as I'm in charge of this case an innocent man has got nothing to worry about." Jack said as he quickly rose and left.

"Damn I thought it was going to be easier then this." The judge said after Jack left. Now that Mr. Benson was living with the boys mother, it was going to be harder to set the boy up. He was going to get his daughter away from that boy no matter what it took. The judge said as he saw Brandy come down the stairs.

It had been two days and Brandy hadn't seen JJ from the time his dad had started living there. She didn't know if it was because of Jack or JJ himself. If it wasn't so far out there she would go see him and find out.

After telling her dad that she was in love with JJ. She was afraid to be seen with him. If her father ever got JJ in his court room, JJ would do a lot of time. She knew that.

Love is a strange thing, Brandy thought. When the only way to prove your love is to let them go. Brandy loved JJ but she was not willing to let him go to prove it. Brandy was afraid that JJ would do something stupid and play right into her dads hands.

Jack was sure that the judge had JJ in his cross hairs. It was obvious that the judge didn't know that JJ was Jacks son. Jack was also sure that the judge was willing to bend the law if it suited him.

"I'll have that bastards gavel before I'm through with him." Jack said to himself as he drove off. He had been in the DEA for about fifteen years and one thing Jack had learned was a lot of friends in the FBI, the CIA more then enough to teach Judge Wells a lesson in justice.

Jack decided the next time he and the judge talked he would be taping every word just in case. He reminded himself that what he was doing wasn't legal either. If this plan worked everyone would be getting what they want. The judge would have a suspect and the case would be closed.

Jack had often thought of seeing Sandy in the lake that misty morning before he left. That memory had gotten him through five years in prison. Jack had decided that when he went fishing he would go to the same place and if he didn't catch any fish he could just sit and picture Sandy in the lake that morning.

Jack made sure that JJ's bike was gone before he pulled up to Tony's trailer. Dan's truck was still there so Jack was sure that Gary was with them. "I thought you might want to test run some pot?" Jack said as he held out a bag and a hundred dollar bill to Tony as he answered the door.

"Well sure! Come on in and join us." Tony said as if him and Jack had been friends for years.

"We'll test run this pot for free Mr. Benson." Gary said as he took the bag of pot to roll a joint.

"Speak for yourself!" Tony said as he put the hundred dollar bill in his pocket.

"I thought you wasn't going to let JJ sell anymore." Dan said.

"That's right! I'm not. I'm going to be doing all the selling from now on. JJ has nothing to do with it."

"In other words you just took over." Dan replied.

"It don't make me no difference who is running the business as long as I get paid." Gary said.

"What I want you boys to do is get the word out that your looking to get rid of a lot of pot for a low price. The catch is they have to take it all at once so they have got to supply the transportation to get rid of it."

"How much are we talking about?" Dan asked still not convinced that Jack could be trusted.

"Beware of strangers baring gifts JJ always said."

"I've got three hundred pounds and I want to get rid of it all. I'll take thirty thousand fat it and they come to a chosen spot to pick it up."

"That sounds cheap enough to me." Gary said. "I wish I had the money. I would buy the pot myself.

"Well unless you got thirty thousand cash, what good is what you wish?"

"This stuff ain't going to knock me out like the last time?" Tony asked.

"I don't know that's why I'm paying you." Jack said.

"Here, shut up and earn your money." Gary said as he handed Tony the joint.

"How much do we get if we find someone to buy all your pot?" Dan asked.

It wasn't hard for Jack to see who did the thinking for this bunch. "I'll give you a thousand dollars a piece Just to set it up between us." Jack said.

The offer brought a smile to Dan's face and Jack was running out of answers. Jack thought Tony was going to say something about JJ's deal until Dan cut him off.

"I've got to be getting home!" Jack said as he started for the door.

"Here's your pot and it sure passed our test." Tony said as he handed Jack the bag.

"Keep it!" Jack said as he walked out.

It was about ten o'clock by the time Jack made it back to Sandy. It wasn't a surprize to Jack that Sandy was angry at him to say the least. No matter how made she was she didn't say a word.

"I'm sorry Sandy. I let time get away from me." Jack said as he came in.

"Jack I know that I can't ask you about your business but I have been worried sick that you and JJ will get hurt playing your games." Jack walked up and took Sandy by the hand.

"Sandy what I'm doing is not some game that men play. Our son and a lot more around here got into something that can get them killed. I may be able to keep JJ from getting killed but the boy might go to prison." Jack thought that Sandy didn't realize until then what danger JJ was in. He thought it best not to tell Sandy that the Judge had his eye on JJ as well.

"I'll run you a bath or you can eat before your bath." Sandy said.

"I'm going to take a long hot bath and then go to bed."

"I'll wait for you." Sandy said as she pointed toward her room.

"Not tonight Sandy, I'm going to bed to sleep."

JJ didn't know if Tony or Dan had gotten a hold of the man they were looking for. I don't like the idea of setting up anyone but it was better if it was a stranger then his friends. If things worked out like JJ planned, he would give the law a man and his friends would slide by.

JJ hadn't know Jack very long but he could tell that he was putting everything he had achieved at risk to save him. JJ had to shake off the thinking or he would have to admit to himself that he liked the man. No that was to close to the word JJ hated so much, love.

It surprised JJ that when he said that word Brandy's face came to his mind. He hadn't gone to see her because of the Judge. Not because JJ was afraid of him, but because JJ had started thinking of what the judge had said to Brandy. 'If you go out with that boy he will take you down with him when he goes.'

Brandy had a future, a life that meant lots of money and high class friends. JJ had always thought of what was best for JJ. Now he could see that the judge was right. Right now he wanted to ride his bike out and pick her up. Drive to the lake and have sex till daylight. Brandy knew how he was when they started going out.

She would get over it he told himself. She will find someone that will give her the life she was meant to have. That's what would happen to her if he got caught trying to set up this man he never seen before.

If things didn't go as planned, he would be as old as Jack before he got out of jail. JJ decided that he would swing by Tony's just to see if he had learned anything about the man. If anyone could find him Tony could. JJ understood why Jack had followed Tony, he knew everybody.

As Jack laid in bed trying to go to sleep, he got JJ on his mind. He knew that the boy wasn't going to let him just come into his life like they had lived their lives together. The boy was twenty years old and Jack would have to treat him like a man. Hell, when you were his age you were serving five years in prison.

It was like Jack was reliving his life all over again. He was just sitting and watching it over again. Jack sat up in bed as if someone had hit him. As he reached over to turn on the lamp, he knocked something to the floor. After Jack got the lamp on, he saw what it was that he had knocked off. It was his old pipe that he had smoked as a boy with the world by the ass.

As Jack looked it over he saw that there was pot still in it. Sandy must have put it there.

"Sandy, I know you meant well. But I'm a law man now I can't be smoking pot." Jack was standing in her doorway in his briefs holding the pipe.

"What are you talking about Jack?" She asked not sure she had heard him right.

"You put this pipe with pot in it, in my room." Jack said.

"I haven't seen that pipe since I gave it to JJ the first time I caught him smoking. Don't go Jack." Sandy said as she patted the bed beside her. If anyone had left the pipe in his room, it had to be JJ.

If JJ had done it it was because he wanted to smoke a piece pipe. Or was it some kind of warning? Jack was wide awake now, so he decided to stay up until JJ got home and find out which one he meant. Jack's eyes fell on Sandy laying there in her thin nightgown. Decided it looked like a good place to wait for JJ. Jack pulled off his briefs and climbed into bed.

JJ was surprised to see Jack and Sandy sitting at the kitchen table as he came in. "Something wrong?" He asked when he saw both Jack and his moms eyes on him.

"Please sit JJ." Jack said as he pointed to the chair across from him. As JJ sat he saw the pipe laying on the table that he had left in Jacks room.

"Did you put this in my room?" Jack asked as he pointed to the pipe.

"Yes I did." JJ said still looking confused as to what was wrong. Jack could tell by the look on JJ's face that he meant no harm.

"I thought you would want it back now that your here." JJ said. "Mom gave it to me a long time ago and I thought you might want it back." JJ said with anger in his voice.

"Don't get mad son." Jack said without thinking. "I'm not acussing you of anything."

"Your not my father! I never had a dad until you came. Did you think I was going to treat you like I have known you all my life?" JJ asked as tears filled his eyes.

Sandy had never seen JJ cry out in the open since he was a teenager.

"I thought you left it so I would smoke pot again with you." A smile crossed JJ's face as he asked Jack if he would have, if he had asked him too.

The smile faded when Jack answered. "No, as long as I'm a DEA agent. I can't."

"And if your not?"

"Then JJ we'll see then." Jack picked up the pipe and put it in his pants pocket.

"Just when I think I've got you figured out, you make me realize I don't know you at all." Sandy said to Jack when JJ left the room. "Would you have smoked with him if you could?"

"Yes!" Was the reply.

JJ was right. Tony was the first to get a hold of the man they were looking for. Dale Cross had stayed at the local restaurant drinking coffee and watching for who was suppose to meet him until the smell of coffee was making him sick.

Dale had work in a big city police force before comming to this small town for a job with the drug force here. Dale had been under cover for the last six months and he was ready for a break. He thought Tony looked like someone he had done buisness with before.

Dale was going to let Tony come to him instead of going over to sit with him. He knew there was another agent working the case and he didn't want to accidentally blow his cover. He didn't know the other agents name or anything like that but he might cross paths with him by accident.

Tony thought it was the man he was looking for but he was just drunk enough that he wasn't sure. If that's him JJ was going to give him a thousand dollars. That was all Tony had on his mind at the time.

"Don't I know you?" Tony asked as he sat down at Dales booth.

"I don't think so." Dale said knowing full well that he had bought off him in the past.

"Sure you do. I'm Tony, Dan and Gary's friend."

"Who's Dan and Gary?" Dale asked as if he didn't know them either.

For a minute Tony thought that he had got the wrong man. "I'm sorry! I thought you was a man that wanted to buy a lot of pot cheap."

Dale knew he had found who he had been waiting for but he hadn't expected him to be so stupid as to talk business there in a restaurant full of people. Dale got up and put a five dollar bill on the table and walked to the door.

As soon as Dale got out the door, Tony picked up the five dollar bill and went to the cash register and told the girl that he wanted to pay his friends bill. Then waited until the girl to give him three dollars back.

Dale waited until he saw Tony come out before he started up his motorcycle. "If you give me a ride home, we can talk about a deal that will make us both rich." Tony said. Without saying anything Dale motioned for Tony to get on behind him with a nod of his head.

Tony had a big smile as he swung his leg over the seat behind Dale. That thousand dollars was his and he was going to get a hold of JJ and collect.

"Okay buddy, here you are." Dale said as the bike came to a stop in front of Tony's trailer.

Tony started talking about everything except the pot deal. So dale stopped him by saying that he didn't have all day.

"Well the deal is three hundred pounds for thirty thousand dollars."

"That sounds good but I'll have to wait a day or so to get the money together." Dale said.

"That'll be ok. I'm going to need a few days to get the pot together myself." Tony explained.

"You mean you don't have the pot yourself?" Dale asked.

"Yes! Yes I have it. But we will need to find a place to make the exchange." Tony thought it best if Dale thought he was the one with the pot. They shook hands and telling each other they would be ready in a couple days. Now all Tony had to do was get ahold of JJ and set up the exchange.

After Dale left, Tony thought of a way he could get a ride out to JJ's. Dan and Gary were nowhere to be found. They were probably out looking for the man Tony had just found. He would need Dan's truck to move the pot once he had set up a deal with JJ.

JJ's dad might be a problem if he finds out that they were going behind his back. "He won't be a problem for long if he gets in my way." Tony said as he reached and pulled out a gun that he kept between the cushion and arm of his chair.

Tony liked the power he felt when he held the gun in his hand. If JJ let him do the exchange, he just might take the money and pot and leave town. Of course he'd have to get rid of any witnesses. He put the gun back in its spot and started walking to JJ's.

Tony hadn't gotten very far when he spotted JJ comming towards him in a hurry. He flaged JJ down and he took Tony home.

"I found him JJ. He said that he would only do buisness with me." Tonyn told JJ.

"That won't work at all."

"Why not?" Tony asked in an angry voice.

"Because I don't want you or Dan or Gary mixed up in this with me." JJ said.

"I'm already mixed in." Tony said. "You need me to make the exchange or he won't buy."

"You just set up the meeting and I'll take it from there." JJ said.

"What about the money you promised?" Tony asked as JJ was about to leave.

"As soon as the deal goes through I'll pay you the money I promised."

"Your going to need a truck to move all that pot." Tony told him.

"I'll talk to Dan and borrow his. I'm sure he will let me use it." JJ replied.

"What about your pa? He will be watching you like a hawk. You won't be able to do anything without him knowing what you are doing." JJ thought for a minute and knew Tony was right.

There would be no way he could get the pot from the old house and get it to the man without Jack knowing what he was doing.

"Ok Tony! I will let you drive the truck to the exchange but as soon as you get the pot there you will have to leave understand." JJ said.

"Sure anything you say JJ. I'll just let you get the money and then we will leave rich men." Tony said with a little laugh.

Tony still had a smile on his face as JJ got on his bike and left to find Dan. The only person that will be leaving that meeting with the pot and the money is me you dumb fuck. With JJ out of the way I'm going to take your pot and your money and your girl.

Tony had always wanted to get into Brandy's pants but she didn't give him a chance with JJ around. Tony laughed out loud to think that with JJ dead she would need his shoulder to cry on. This seemed so easy that Tony was surprised that he hadn't thought of it before now.

JJ hadn't wanted to get Tony mixed up in this but he knew that he would be able to do everything by himself. All he would have to do is make Tony get out of there before the law came. Dan's truck was sitting at the bar so JJ stopped and went in. Dan and Gary were sitting at a table in the back.

Jack had got word that the Judge wanted to see him, so he went to see he wanted. The judge told Jack that contact had been made with the undercover agent. He also told Jack the man who was setting up the deal was Tony. Jack breathed a sigh of relief that it wasn't JJ. Jack knew that JJ was behind the deal but the judge didn't.

"I'm sorry that I accused that Tall boy. I know that you and his mother are living together." The Judge said as he stuck out his hand for Jack to shack.

"I think the boy comes from good stook." Jack said as he shook the Judges hand.

"I'm sure you do!" The Judge said with a wink.

It surprised Jack that the judge didn't know that JJ was his son. He was sure that Brandy would have told her father by now. All Jack had to do now was set up the exchange and as soon as the agent took possession of the pot he would bust him.

The bust would make Jack look like a fool and he would quit the DEA in shame but his son and his buddies would stay out of jail. They hadn't set up the exchange yet so he still had time to stop JJ from going through with it. As Jack came out to his car, Brandy was standing by it.

"Please Mr. Benson will you take this to JJ?" She asked and handed him a sealed envelope.

"Yes! I will give it to him for you. I want to thank you for not telling the Judge that JJ is my son." Jack said as he took the letter from her.

"I love JJ! And I don't understand why he stopped coming to see me?" Brandy said as tears came to her eyes.

"I'm sure he is only doing what he thinks is best for you."

"I just wish everybody would stop doing what they think is best for me." Brandy said as she turned and went back into the house crying.

"I wonder if Sandy cried like that when I left her so many years ago."

When Jack got back home, he learned that JJ had gone out toward the old house with someone in a truck.

"What's going on Jack?" Sandy asked as Jack took out his gun and stuck it in his belt behind his back before he walked out the door.

Sandy ran out and caught him by the arm. "Sandy you just have to trust me and go back in the house.

"How can I trust you if you won't tell me why you have to take a gun to talk to our son." Sandy said with tears in her eyes. Jack put his arms around Sandy and kissed her.

"The gun is so me or JJ won't get hurt." Jack said as he got in his car and headed to the old house.

Jack stopped the car just before the old house came into sight. Dan's truck was backed up to the door and JJ and Tony were putting the pot in the back. JJ and Tony were the only people that Jack saw so he knew that they hadn't made the exchange yet. If he did anything now he would be screwed.

Jack didn't know where they were going to meet the other agent so he would have to follow them to find out. Jack hurried back to his car and drove out to the highway before JJ could see him.

He would wait until they came out before he started following them. It was getting dark by the time the truck passed where he was sitting. Jack followed the truck to a dirt road just outside of an empty house before it stopped.

JJ had come up behind him on his bike so Jack just kept on going as the bike turned onto the road as well. As soon as he could Jack turned around and started back to the road. As soon as he started to turn onto the road another motorcycle pulled into the road so Jack kept on going again. From the way the tall grass grew in the middle of the road Jack could tell that the road wasn't used very often.

Tony was sitting in the truck smoking a joint as JJ pulled up on his bike. "I'll take over from here." JJ said as he told Tony to take his bike and leave.

"I told you he won't do the deal with anyone but me!" Tony yelled as he came out of the truck.

"Well he'll just have to deal with me or there won't be a deal." JJ said getting very angry at Tony for not doing what they had agreed to.

The sound of the other bike got both JJ's and Tony's attention as it came toward where they were. "Damn!" JJ said as he thought he would have more time to get rid of Tony before the man arrived. Tony came up behind JJ who was looking in the direction of the sound. Tony pulled out the gun and hit JJ in the back of the head as hard as he could.

JJ fell to the ground out cold. Tony was going to shot JJ but realized that the sound of the gun would scare off the man before he got the money. He would shoot JJ after he got the money and kill that man at the same time.

Tony had just gotten the bike and JJ dragged to the bushes before Dale pulled up. "I have the pot!" Tony said as he pointed toward the truck. "Do you have the money?"

"Yes, I have it." Dale said as he pulled out a thick brown envelope.

"Well let me have it." Tony said as he reached for the envelope.

"Not so fast!" Dale said as he put the envelope back into his pocket.

"Wait for what?" Tony asked.

"I'm going to make sure you don't have a truck load of yard grass before I give you the money."

"Okay, Okay, go over there and see for yourself." Tony said as he pointed to the truck.

Dale got off the bike and walked to the back of the truck. He had to make sure that it was pot before the bust would stick.

"Now let me see the money." Tony demanded as he came up behind Dale.

"This is pot alright Tony, but I'm afraid that you are under arrest." Dale said as he turned around. To his surprise Tony was pointing a gun at him.

"I don't think so !" Tony said as he shot Dale at point blank range. The bullet hit dale in the chest knocking him to the ground. "You fucking law dog! Tony said as he pointed the gun at Dales head. Dale thought he was a dead man before he could get to his own gun.

Dale heard the sound of a gun going off but didn't feel any pain. The sound rang out again and the gun fell from Tony's hand as he fell to the ground. A tall man stepped up and stood at Tony's side. The vest that Dale had put on had saved his life so to speak. Dale didn't know if the man was there with Tony or not. As Dale reached for his gun the tall man told him he was DEA.

You could hear the sigh of relief come from Dale as he dropped his gun. The man seemed to be looking for something or someone as Dale got to his feet only to sit back down.

The man who had shot Tony walked into the bushes and came back with another boy in his arms and laid him in the light of the bike Dale could see that the man was crying as he knelt beside the boy. There was blood all over the mans shirt and at first Dale thought he might be shot too. The sound of sirens coming surprised both Jack and Dale. As far as they knew, no one knew that they were there. Jack had parked the car a good piece down the road. He needed to get JJ to the hospital as fast as he could after he felt a pulse.

The first police car that stopped Jack jerked open the door and put JJ in the back. The officer driving was not sure what was going on when Jack told him to to get them to the hospital. The Judge came up to the car and told the officer to do what Jack had told him to do. With the lights and sirens going the car pulled away.

Jack had thought that JJ had been shot in the head until the doctors told him that the boy had only been knocked in the head with the gun. Jack was sure it wasn't to bad if that was all that happened to him. The doctors changed his mind when he told Jack that the boy was in a coma and he might not come out of it if the brain was damaged.

While the doctors worked on JJ, Jack stood in the waiting room. Judge Wells came to the hospital. "How did you know where to find us?" Jack asked.

"JJ called and told us to watch for a man and a truck out there. We didn't know where until we heard the gun shots. I didn't know you had the boy working for you." The judge said. "Until he called and told us where to look for the man and the truck. How is the boy?"

"They don't know yet if my son will make it." Jack said. Judge Wells couldn't hide the surprise look on his face when he heard Jack call JJ his son.

"I sent a car to get the boys mother and bring her here. The under cover agent told us how you saved his life."

"My boy saved his life if he hadn't lead me there your man would be dead."

"We'll have to give him a hero's plaque or something." The Judge said.

"You pompass bastard, you first wanted to frame JJ. Now you want to give him a piece of wood that says thank you on it after he got his brains beat in." Jack stepped back away from the Judge before he put the judge in the bed next to his son. "Your daughter gave me this to give to JJ because she loves him." Jack said as he pulled the envelope covered in JJ's blood from his shirt pocket. "She told JJ how much she loves him before he became a hero. You best keep your plaque and get the fuck out of my face."

"There's no need for you to talk to me like that." The judge said as he left.

The police car hadn't even got to a complete stop before Sandy jumped out and ran into the hospital. She could tell by the look on Jacks face that the news wasn't good.

"Is my baby dead?" Sandy asked as she came toward Jack.

"No Sandy. He isn't dead but he may be in a coma for a long time." Jack said as he put his arms around her. "I'm going to get the best doctors I can to help him."

"Where were you Jack when he needed your help?" Sandy cried as she broke from Jacks arms. "It's your help that got him put here in the first place." Sandy cried as she slapped Jack in the face.

Tears came from Jacks eyes not because of the slap, but because he knew she was right. It was the first time in Sandy's life that she saw Jack cry like a baby. Sandy put her arms around Jack and they both cried together.

It was two hours before the doctor came and told them that they had done everything they could for JJ. He was in a room on life support. The sound of the heart monitor and breathing devices was the only sound Jack and Sandy heard as they went into the room.

JJ's head was wrapped like a turban as he lay motionless. "Why don't you go home and clean up." Sandy told Jack as she pointed to his blood stained shirt. "I'll stay here with JJ while you get some rest."

Jack had forgot that his car was still out where he had left it. "My car isn't here and I don't have a ride." Jack replied. The words had no sooner came out of Jacks mouth when a very grateful Dale came into the room.

"Mr. Benson I would like to thank you for saving my life!" Dale said. "I'm sorry about your boy." Pointing towards JJ.

"I was just doing my job." Jack said as he shook Dales hand.

"Well thank you for doing your job."

"Are you thankful enough to give him a ride to his car?" Sandy asked.

"Sure I would be glad to give you a ride." Dale said. "It'll give you a chance to explain a few things about tonight, that I'm confused about."

"What kind of questions?" Jack asked.

"Well to start with, What was your boy doing out there to begin with?"

"He was working for me on this case." Jack said as he looked at JJ.

"I knew that they had another agent working a different angle but I didn't know that there were two of you."

"I'm really not in the mood to answer a bunch of questions." Jack said.

"That's ok! I was just curious." Dale said as the two of them left the room.

Dale must have thanked Jack a hundred times before he dropped Jack off at the car. Once Jack got back home and took a bath he tried to get some sleep. The thought of JJ laying in that hospital bed stopped him from getting any sleep.

Jacks thoughts went all the way back to when he had left home under the belief that he had killed his pa. Only to find out that his pa didn't die by his hands. But by some bad moonshine a year or two later. He thought of David and Shafoun who took an overdose on LSD and died. It seemed to Jack that anytime he got close to anyone they turned up dead.

Now his son, that he hadn't known about, is laying brain dead in a hospital. He was afraid that Sandy would be next. That thought made him get up and turn on the light. As he sat on the side of the bed, he noticed the pipe laying on his nightstand. Jack reached for the pipe and fired it up.

The pot was so strong that it made him cough so hard he had to put it back down. It had been twenty years since he had smoked and he got stoned off that one hit. Just like the first time.

Sandy was asleep on the cot the doctor had put in JJ's room when Brandy came into the room. As Sandy woke up, Brandy was bent over JJ kissing his head.

"Is he going to be okay?' Brandy asked as she noticed Sandy's eyes were open.

"They don't know yet." Sandy said as she got up and walked around to where Brandy was standing.

"My dad told me how he was a hero and that his dad, Mr. Benson, shot and killed the bastard that did this to him."

"I tried talking to him but got no reaction." Sandy said as she laid her hand on JJ's.

"If you would like to go home and get some rest, I'll sit with him." Brandy said.

"How kind of you but I want to wait until the doctor comes in to examine him." Sandy said. The two girls sat down and waited for the doctor together. As they sat and talked Sandy could tell that Brandy was in love with JJ. The way she had been in love with Jack so long ago.

Brandy was telling Sandy how JJ hated for her to tell him that she loved him. They were both laughing when Jack came through the door. "What's so funny?"

"Oh, we are just having a little girl talk." Sandy said as she got up and kissed Jack.

Jack walked over to where JJ laid and patted him on the shoulder saying "I love you son." which started both women laughing again. Jack didn't understand why him telling his son that he loved him could be so funny. He looked at the two laughing women but didn't say anything.

The doctor came in and made them all leave while he checked JJ's progress. All three of them waited for the doctor to come out and answer their questions.

"No change." Was all he could tell them. "It's up to JJ now. We have done all we can do." The doctor said as he started to walk away. "You can try talking to him, sometimes it will help. Just don't get your hopes to high."

"Hope is all we have." Sandy said as the doctor left. The three of them went back into the room and Sandy tried to hold back her tears but couldn't.

"Why don't you take her home so she can get some rest." Brandy said as she stood beside Jack. "I'll stay here with JJ and if there is any change, I'll call."

"Are you sure?" Brandy nodded her head yes and Jack put his arm around Sandy and lead her towards the door.

"I want to stay here with my baby." Sandy said as Jack just guided her on out saying that if she didn't get some rest he would have two people in the hospital. Sandy was to tired to protest. "What do you think of Brandy?" Sandy asked as Jack was driving them home.

"I think she cares for JJ very much." Jack said as he remembered Brandy giving him that letter to give to JJ.

"She loves him the way I love you." Sandy said as she patted his leg.

"You know that I've got loose ends to clear up before this case is over." Jack said as he put his hand over Sandy's and gently squeezed.

"I thought it was over after you killed the bastard that did this to JJ?"

"The other boys that were in this with him. I just can't let them go."

"Jack please let it go! I would die if something happened to you like what happened to JJ, Or even worse. You promised you were going to quit as soon as this case was over."

"I know Sandy. What I told you and what I'm going to do just that as soon as I get the others."

"What others?" Sandy asked as she jerked her hand free.

"I don't believe that Tony was the one behind what he did."

"He was the only one out there besides you and that Dale, wasn't he?" Sandy asked.

"Well yes. But if.."

"If a cow had wings it could fly." Sandy said before he could finish.

"Don't you want to get all of them that did this to JJ?"

"I want you to let it go before I lose you too." Sandy cried.

Jack knew he didn't have any proof that Dan and Gary was involved in what Tony did. But if they were he was going to find out. The rest of the ride home was made in silence. Sandy knew that Jack wasn't going to give it up, no matter what she said.

She had JJ for twenty years and Jack had only known him for a week. She wasn't about to take a chance on him getting himself killed even if she had to tie him up and lock him in his room.

"Please come in and lay down with me until I go to sleep?" She asked as they pulled up to the house.

"You won't get any sleep if I laid down with you." Jack said with a little laugh.

"Please Jack!" Sandy begged as she put her hand on his thigh and squeezed.

"Ok! Jack said as he shut off the car. Now all I gotta do is keep him in bed. Sandy thought as she got out of the car. At least until I think of something else.

Jack hadn't gotten much sleep the night before so the idea of getting some rest wasn't such a bad idea. He lead the way into the house with Sandy behind him. He walked to Sandy's room without looking back. He was surprised when he did look back because Sandy had started taking off her clothes at the door. She was down to her panties by the time Jack looked back.

"You sure are in a hurry to get into bed!" Jack said with a stuned look on his face.

"Yes but not to sleep!" Sandy said as she pushed jack onto the bed fully clothed. Sex wasn't what Jack had on his mind when he had went into the bedroom. The sight of Sandy's nude body soon brought it to mind. It amazed him how Sandy's body looked as firm as when she was twenty. For a forty year old women she looked pretty good. Sandy laid down beside him and started unbuttoning his shirt.

"Your sure?" Jack asked as Sandy worked to get the last button.

"I'm sure!" Sandy said as she started undoing Jacks belt. Sandy hadn't gotten the belt completely open before she lifted Jacks leg to untie his shoe. Jack started to get concerned when Sandy didn't even untie his other shoe before pulling it off.

"Slow down girl!" Jack said as he took Sandy by the wrists and pulled her down beside him. Sandy put both hands over her eyes trying to hide her tears. "Why are you crying?" Jack asked as he propped himself on one elbow beside her.

"I don't know!" Sandy cried as she wiped the tears from her eyes.

"You are the only one who does!" Jack said as his sock feet hit the floor.

"Please Jack don't go! I need you to hold me!" Sandy said as she rose to her knees on the bed.

"If that is what you want then why the tears?"

"It's just so much has happened that I'm afraid of losing everyone I love!"

"I know you've been through a lot in the past twenty four hours. I'm sorry but you should know that I been through a lot myself."

Sandy lowered her head and looked down at Jacks sock feet. She thought of how she had been thinking of herself and her pain. She had not stopped to think how Jack must be feeling. "I'm sorry Jack! I have been thinking of myself only. I know you are more hurt then me. You didn't even know you had a son until a week ago."

"Look we are both tired so I'm going so you can get some rest." Jack said as he picked up his things. The tears started for real when Sandy laid back down. This time Sandy was crying for Jack and not herself.

As Jack was putting his shoes back on the phone rang. It was Dale on the other end. "Jack your name came up when we were interrogating the boy that owns the truck that Tony was driving. I think you need to come down here and straighten it out." He said then hung up the phone.

Jacks mind was racing to think of anything that Dan could tell them that he couldn't cover by his job. He hadn't tied his shoe's or buttoned his shirt by the time he sat in his car. All the way to the homicide department Jack tried to think of any single word that he could have said that he might have trouble covering. He did his best to act as natural as he could as he entered the police station.

"That's him! That's him right there!" Gary said pointing in Jacks direction. Gary's fluffy afro looked like a helmet as the blond curls reached down half his back. His piercing green eyes locked on Jack.

"What's going on here?" Jack asked as he entered the room the three were sitting in. Dale rose from his chair and guided Jack across the hall to another room.

"The boy is saying you was in on the sell of the pot that Tony had on Dan's truck."

"That's ridiculous! I was the head agent that broke the case." Jack said with a shocked look on his face.

"I know!" Dale said. "I just wanted you to know what he was saying before it went any higher up."

"I know him." Gary said as Dale and Jack came back into the room.

"Yes. I've seen you before but you were with that Tony and Gary if my memory serves me right." Jack said as he sat in a chair across from Gary.

"No I'm Gary. You are talking about Dan."

"This Dan fellow, he the one that owns the truck?" Jack asked as if he didn't know.

"Yes! Yes that's him."

"What is your involvement in this attempted murder of a police officer?" Jack asked Gary, who sat back in his chair in shock when he realized that Jack was a law man.

"No! I didn't try to kill anyone!" Gary yelled as both and Dale were looking at him. "I didn't know Tony was in it until I heard about him getting himself killed."

"Didn't you ask him what he wanted the truck for?"

"That's Dan's truck. I have nothing to do with who he lets drive it."

"Why don't you tell Mr. Benson of the DEA what you are saying about him."

"All I said was that he told me and Dan that he was going to be the only man in town to get your pot."

"Where were we when I told you that?"

"We were at Tony's trailer." Gary said.

"And you saw me give that pot to on Dan's truck to him?"

"No, I didn't say that. I said you probably sold it to him." Gary said.

"Have you checked his aliby?" Jack asked Dale.

"He said that him and this Dan were in the Black Cat bar so drunk they couldn't leave let alone be involved in the deal. And from the way he tells it. I believe him."

"Well believe me when I tell you that I had nothing to do with that deal between you and Tony. For God sake, I was the one who told the Judge to put you back on the case. I had to many people who needed watching." Jack said.

"I know Jack. That's why I called you. I'm going to cut him loose and let it go. We couldn't get a judge to hear the case when we checked the bar the two were at."

Jack smiled and shook Dales hand before he walked out. Now I can let it go Sandy. Jack thought to himself as he started up his car and headed toward home and Sandy. Tomorrow he would get in touch with his office in D.C. and get the paper work started on his retirement.

Sandy must have cried herself to sleep because she was laying in nothing but her panties on top of the bed spread with her face buried in her pillow. Jack steped back out into the hall and made his way to the bath tub.

Jack turned the water on so the tub could fill while he got some clothes to put on from his room. Jacks eyes fell on the half smoked pipe that he had put back on his night stand. He pulled out the drawer and put the pipe out of sight before he returned to the bathroom. As Jack approached the bathroom he could hear that the water stopped running.

"How thoughtful of you to run me a bath." Sandy said as Jack entered the room. Sandy had her back to Jack so he tossed his clothed on the seat of the comodeand started taking off his clothes.

"It's over Sandy, it's all over." Jack said as he came up behind Sandy and put his arms around her waist. He pulled her back against him so she couldn't turn around. Sandy could tell from Jacks erect penis that he didn't have any clothes on. She could feel it through her thin panties that he was nude.

As Sandy bent over to pull off her panties, Jack stood right where he was and Sandys hips were forced back into his erect penis. Sandy closed her eyes and put her hands on the rim of the tub then stepped back forcing Jacks penis even further between her thighs. Her fingers turned white from the grip she had on the tub.

"Ohh!" escape her lips as Jack found his target.

"We both will need a bath before I'm through." Jack said as he thrust forward again. He was right by the time he was finished both him and Sandy got in the tub.

Jack sat with his back against the tub and Sandy sat between his legs. Her head on his chest while he told her his plans for their future.

"I win again." Jack and Sandy could hear Brandy say as they came in JJ's room. Brandy had bought a checker game and set it on JJ's chest. She would raise his hand and put his finger on a checker and move it to where she wanted, then put his hand down and make her move.

Brandy had won ten straight games. Jack and Sandy both burst out laughing. Jack stopped laughing as he walked to JJ's side and laid his hand on JJ's bandaged head.

"We are here waiting on you to come back to us son." Brandy smiled as she picked up the checker board and moved to the chair.

"I wonder where he is at?" Sandy asked as she placed her right hand on

Jacks shoulder and laid her head on his arm.

"The ultimate buzz." Jack said with his eyes fixed on JJ.

"Has there been any change at all?" Sandy asked Brandy as she raised her head.

Brandy said no as she shook her head at the same time. "I've been talking to him like the doc said. He didn't even make a move when I told him how much I love him. If any of that had gotten through he would have moved."

"I'm sure he knows dear." Sandy said as she went and sat down.

"I'll be back later son." Jack said as he brought the back of his fingers down across JJ's cheek. "Brandy would you like a ride home, seeing as to how I'm going there?" Jack said as he turned to leave.

"Yes Mr. Benson." Brandy said as she shoved the checker game to Sandy. "He's easy to beat."

"From now on you can call me Jack." Jack said after looking at Sandy. "I'll be back soon Sandy. I just need to get a report from the Judge." They were gone before she could say 'Okay sweetheart.' Sandy didn't like the feeling she got in her stomach. Jack is just being kind, I hope.

"Mr. Benson did you ever give JJ that letter?" Brandy asked as Jack pulled out of the hospital parking lot.

"I'm sorry Brandy, it slipped my mind with all that's happened. It's laying on my dresser and if you want it back. I'll bring it to you." Jack said without taking his eyes off the traffic.

"No, I don't want it back. There are a few things in there that I just as soon JJ didn't read when he comes back to us. If you could just burn it?" Brandy asked.

"Sure I'll be glad to." Jack said as he winked at Brandy.

"Thank you Mr. Benson."

"I told you to call me Jack. I think we are good enough friends that you don't have to call me Mr. Benson anymore."

"I don't think that Sandy would like it. Do you?"

"I'm old enough to be your father. I don't think that Sandy is going to be to upset about who can call me by my name." Jacks laughter was filled with doubt.

"Ok, Jack it is." Brandy said as she patted him on the arm.

"Can I ask you a personal question Jack?"

A puzzled look came to Jacks face as he told her "Sure."

Without hesitation Brandy asked. "When did you know for sure that you were in love with Sandy?" A small grin came to Jacks face as he realized that Brandy was coming to him for advice instead of the Judge.

"I'm not sure when. I woke up one morning and I knew that I was in love with Sandy. Back when we first met I was on the run from the law. So I knew that the law would catch up with me. I loved her then but I couldn't tell her because she would end up getting hurt so I didn't tell her.

"I think that's what JJ is doing to me." Brandy said with great excitement.

Jack was glad to see the Judges house come into view. Now he could get rid of Brandy and all her questions.

"You will burn that letter for me?" Brandy said as she opened the car door and got out.

"Sure Brandy. I'll get rid of it for you."

Jack had to listen to the judge apologize for five minutes before he got to tell the judge why he was there. He had to get a statement from him that the case was considered closed. Jack was surprised when after the judge learned that Jack was retiring from the DEA. His face had a grin from ear to ear.

"How would you like to be our county sherriff?"

"I thought there was an elction for that job?"

"Sure theres going to be an election but Sherriff Brown is on his way out and there wouldn't be much compotitionfor a man with your record."

"I thank you for the offer but I'm getting completely out of being a law man."

Sandy stood looking out at the parking lot hoping to see Jack as he pulled in. She had spent the most part of her first hour talking to JJ and telling him how she hoped that Jack wasn't having sex with Brandy. She could never have talked to JJ like that if he hadn't been unconscious.

"Oh good!" Sandy said as she saw Jacks car pull in."Now you behave yourself." She told JJ before Jack made it to the room.

Doctor Stringer stopped Jack in the hall and told him that he should take Sandy home. That she wasn't doing JJ any good by just sitting in his room. Sandy met Jack at the door as he came into the room.

"How's he doing?" Jack asked.

"There has been no change." Sandy said as they both looked in JJ's direction.

"well get your things together so we can go home." Jack told her. "I'm not going anywhere." Sandy said.

"Yes you are. Your going home with me." Jack said. From the way he was talking to her she knew he was going to take her home, even if he had to pack her away from there. "The doctor asked me to get you out of here and by God that's what I'm going to do."

Sandy knew that to cause a scene in the hospital would do nobody any good. So she did as Jack had asked. As the two of them reached home, Sandy noticed that the jacket Jack had been wearing the night JJ got hurt was laying in his back seat. Sandy reached and picked it up as she got out.

The jacket still had blood on it and a blood covered envelope fell from the pocket and hit the ground. As she picked it up she noticed that the envelope was blank. Sandy started to tell Jack about it then decided not to. She folded the jacket over the letter and walked in the house. Jack went straight to the fridge and got a cold beer before he sat down.

"I'm going to put this jacket in the laundry." Sandy told Jack as she went up stairs.

Sandy opened the letter and looked at the signature at the bottom, love Brandy was what it said. Her eyes jumped back to the beging of the letter.

I know that I haven't known you very long but I have fallen in love with you. I think that my dad might suspect that there is is something between us. All I can think about is when we made love the first time by the lake. I can't wait until we can make love all we want. Love Brandy. Sandy was in shock as she sat down on Jacks bed.

The dirty bastard is fucking that little whore. Right behind my back. Sandy was thinking about going down stairs and telling that son of a bitch to get his ass out of her house. Now just slow down Sandy. She told herself. He didn't open the letter, so she decided to wait and see if Jack told her about the letter before she asked him about it. As soon as she got more information then she would let him have it.

Sandy put the letter back into the envelope and placed it on Jacks dresser. Jack was sitting, listening to music and drinking a cold beer when Sandy came into the room. She sits down beside him on the couch.

"What have you been doing?" Jack asked as he put his arm around her shoulders.

"I was in your room getting laundry ready to wash." Sandy replied not taking her eyes off of Jack as she spoke.

"You can do the wash tomorrow while I'm gone." Jack told her as he took a drink of beer.

"Where are you going tomorrow?" Sandy asked in a louder voice then she intended. In all the years that Jack had lived with other women, he had never let one of them question his movements.

"I'm going to take care of my business." Jack said loudly. "Whats bothering you Sandy?" Jack asked as he took his arm from around her shoulders.

"I just want you to spend more time with me." Sandy said as she put his arm back around her shoulders.

"As soon as I get my retirement started I promise you that I'll spend more time with you." Jack said as he kissed her. As soon as the kiss ended Jack rose from the couch.

"I'm going to take a bath and do a favor for a friend." Jack said as he walked off. Sandy was on her feet and followed him upstairs.

"You run the bath water while I go get some clean clothes to put on." Jack said as he left Sandy in the bathroom. She turned the water on in the tub then tipped toed into Jacks door before she stopped.

Jack was standing at his dresser holding the letter between his fingers and setting it on fire. The bastard was destroying evidence. Sandy thought. She was surprised at how close the flames came to his hand before he put it in the ashtray. Sandy turned back to the tub and was taking off her clothes when Jack came back in the bathroom.

"What are you doing?" Jack asked as he entered the room.

"I was going to take a bath with you." Sandy said standing there in her panties.

"Sandy I just want to take a bath and go to bed, not have sex."

"We don't have to have sex." Sandy said in a loud angry voice.

"Ok, ok. I don't feel like making love." Jack said trying to make amends for saying sex instead of making love.

"Jack is there another woman in your life?" Sandy asked as she reached and picked up her things off the floor.

"No Sandy there is not anyone in my life but you and JJ." Jack said as he put his arms around Sandy. "What about the letter from Brandy saying how much she loves you and the sex you had by the lake?"

"What are you talking about?" Jack asked as he backed up from Sandy.

"The letter you just burned up." She said pointing to Jacks room.

"That letter was for JJ and I didn't open it like you did." Jack said angrily.

Sandy put her hand to her mouth trying to stop the words but realized it was to late.

"You thought me and Brandy are having an affair?"

"Well it was your jacket and you did burn it." Sandy said as the tears started coming to her eyes. Jack was laughing so hard that he couldn't talk so he just pointed his finger. "What are you laughing about?" Sandy asked as she started slapping at the air.

Jack was at no risk getting slapped because Sandy was a good five feet away. "Brandy gave me that letter to give to JJ before he got hurt. But I didn't get the chance to give it to him." Jack said when he got his laughter under control.

It's hard to describe how foolish Sandy felt once she realized how much she had let her mind put all the clues in the wrong place. "I'm sorry Jack. I was so afraid that I was going to lose you again."

"I'm starting to think that I made a mistake in thinking we could just pick up where we left off so many years ago." Jack said.

"No, Jack. It's it's not like that. I was wrong and I admit it but don't leave me please." Sandy said as she dropped the clothes she was holding and ran to Jack and put her arms around him. "I love you so much is why I did it."

Jack put his arms back around Sandy and pulled her even closer. "Sandy I've been in love with you from the morning I saw you in the lake. I have had other women in my life but none could take you out of my mind. If you want my love the first thing you've got to do is trust me." Jack said as he squeezed Sandy tighter.

"Oh Jack! I promise you that I will never doubt you again. I will never be jealous of another women if you just forgive me." Sandy said as she squeezed Jack's waist.

"I'll forgive you this time but if it happens again, I'm gone."

"What about your bath?" Sandy asked as Jack picked Sandy up in his arms and headed toward his room.

"I'll need a bath more in about thirty minutes." Jack said as he kept on walking with Sandy in his arms. The two of them made love as if they were teenagers. Sandy was sure she would have gotten pregnant if she wasn't thirty eight years old. The thought frightened her at first but the more she thought about it she pictured a little girl crawling around the house.

Sandy placed her hand on her stomach. There was no reason she couldn't have another baby. Everything still worked it just got more dangerous at her age was all. I wonder what Jack would think about it she asked herself as Jack got up and went to take his bath. Your just being silly she told herself as she laid back on the bed.

Jack was in the tub when Sandy got up and came into the bathroom. "What do you think about about us having a baby?" Sandy asked as she stood by the tub.

"Don't be silly Sandy. We are to old to have a baby and start all over again." Jack said as he stood up to get out of the tub.

"My mom was in her late thirties when she had me." Sandy said.

"Maybe I should start using protection." Jack said as he dried off.

"No Jack that won't do at all. It's a sin against God to do that." Sandy said in a frightened voice.

"Okay. As long as your health isn't in danger, we won't use birth control. I didn't know you were a bible thumper." Jack said with a little laugh.

"I'm no bible thumper. I know we were put here on earth to have as many kids as we can." Jack stopped laughing when he saw how serious the look on Sandy's face was.

Religion was one subject Jack didn't want to get started on. His mom was a full fledged bible thumper from way back. Even now when he thought of her she was quoting a verse from the bible.

It was six o'clock in the morning, Jack and Sandy were asleep in her bed room when the phone rang. It was the RN from the hospital saying that JJ was coming out of his coma. They should come right down.

Both were dressed and standing in JJ's room with in an hour. The doctor told them that he was consious but he had amnesia from the brain damage. He didn't seem to know anyone or how he got to the hospital.

"I'm his mother, He'll know me." Sandy said as she rushed to JJ's side. JJ's eyes made him look like a frightened animal. "Baby it's me, mommy." Sandy said as she took JJ's hand in hers. JJ jerked back his hand and let out a little grunt as he did. "What's wrong with him Jack?" Sandy asked as she took a step back.

"Sandy he don't remember who he is let alone you." Jack said as stepped between JJ and Sandy. Jack got quit a shock when JJ reached for his hand. He wasn't sure what JJ was going to do when he grabbed Jacks hand and pulled him closer.

"Doctor, what's he doing? He hasn't known Jack but for a week before the accident." Sandy asked.

"He can see that his dad looks just like him. So he feels safe with him. As Jack sat down on the side of the bed JJ through his arms around Jacks neck and laid his bandaged head on his arm. It half way made Sandy mad when the doctor ran everyone out of the room except Jack.

"Everythings going to be alright now." Jack said as he put his arms around his son for the first time. When JJ tried to talk you could tell that he had no control over his tongue and he could not form his words.

"Do you know who I am?" Jack asked as he held JJ in his arms.

"Papa." JJ managed to say.

A smile came to Jack's face as he said. "If that's what you want to call me."

"Papa." JJ said again.

"Ok, ok. Papa it is."

The doctor had told her to wait in the hall until Jack came to get her. She had been sure that he would be right out to get her, but when she had been waiting for twenty minutes she rushed into the room.

"It's ok JJ. This is your mother." Jack said. Sandy approached JJ like he was a frightened bunny. This time JJ didn't jerk his hand back when Sandy took it in hers. The nurse came through the door with a tray of food.

"You folks will have to go while I take out his Iv and get him on some solid food." The nurse said.

"Can we just sit over there and be quiet?" Sandy asked.

"No I'm afraid you will need to leave the room for at least thirty minutes.

"We'll be back son, in a little while. So you do what the nice lady tells you, ok?" Jack asked as he got up off the bed. JJ grunted then shook his head yes.

"Mommy will be right back." Sandy said as her and Jack walked out the door.

"Something to eat sounds good to me." Jack said as he and Sandyleft JJ's room.

"I could stand to eat something." Sandy said as she took Jacks hand in hers and started down the hall. "what did you and JJ talk about papa?" Sandy asked as her and Jack sat down at the table in the canteen.

"JJ can only shake his head for now but you give him a few weeks and and he'll be talking like old times." Jack said as he sat down.

"Lets hope not." Sandy said which surprised Jack.

"What do you mean?" Jack asked in a high toned voice.

"Well sugar if he starts talking to you like old times, you will want to whip his ass." Sandy said with a laugh. Jack thought about it for a few seconds then started laughing too. "You know that he is a completely different person then he was when he came in here, don't you?" Sandy asked as her laughing stopped.

"I know what your saying Sandy. I can't discribe how it made me feel when JJ put his arms around my neck and then call me papa."

"I know exactly what you felt Jack. I felt the same way when he looked at me while he was sucking my breastand smiled."

"Sandy that's what I'm talking about. I wasn't here for that kind of stuff. This is the first time in my life that I felt like a father for JJ. What frightens me is that he will get his memory back enough that he will know that he hates me."

Sandy put her hand on Jacks arm and with a smile she said."If it's not broke, don't fix it."

"I know your right. I was never one to look a gift horse in the mouth." Jack said right before he kissed Sandy.

"There is a hotel a few blocks down." The waitress said as she laid our menus on the table.

"It's quit alright, Miss Mary. We are married." Jack said as he held up Sandy's hand and showed Mary her ring.

"Maybe so, but to each other?" Mary asked.

Sandy was on her way to standing up when Jack stuck out his arm to stop her. "Young lady if you like working here instead of being in a room up stairs, you will get us another waitress." Jack said in an angry voice.

"Is something wrong?" A short chubby man asked as he approached their table.

"You bet your ass there's a problem. This bitch just accused me of being a whore and I don't like it." Sandy said as she pointed her finger in Mary's direction.

"Is this true Mary?" The short chubby man asked.

"I just told you what she said and now your calling me a liar." Sandy shouted at the top of her voice.

"No mam I'm not saying anything like that. Mary you go to my office and I'll get you people a new waitress." The short chubby man said as he motioned for a different waitress.

"I just lost my appetite." Sandy said as she headed out leaving Jack at the table.

"Do you think we should call Brandy and tell her about JJ?" Jack asked when he caught up with Sandy.

"He don't know me yet. Do you think he will remember her?" Sandy asked

"I don't know, I didn't read the letter." Jack said. "That was a cheap shot, even for you Jack."

"You are afraid that he will remember someone else and not you." Jack said in a voice that lets you know he was getting pissed. Sandy knew that he was right and started backing down.

"I'll call her." Sandy said and walked to a phone.

Jack caught the doctor as he came out of JJ's room. "How much can he remember?"

"Not much but he may wake up tomorrow and remember everything. It's possible that he may never remember." I'm back to square one, Jack thought as the doctor went on down the hall.

A smile came to JJ's face as Jack came into his room. JJ grunted and patted the bed beside him.

"Tell me son, how much you remember about the accident?" JJ looked at him with a puzzled look on his face. "I'm going to ask you some questions and you just shake your head if you know who I'm talking about." JJ nodded his head yes for him to go ahead.

"Do you know who I am?" Jack asked pointing to himself. JJ nodded yes and said papa.

"Yes that's right. Now do you know a boy named Tony?" No was the response JJ gave.

"Do you know a boy named Dan?" No was JJ's answer.

"Do you know a girl named Brandy?" No was JJ's response.

Sandy came through the door before Jack could ask anymore questions. "Do you know who that is JJ?" JJ paused before he answered no.

"I'm your mother JJ, don't you even know your mother?" Sandy asked.

"Ma." JJ said as Sandy rushed to his other side.

"There is someone on her way over to see you." Sandy said as she sat down beside JJ. "Brandy will be here in a few minutes. She couldn't believe that you came out of a coma and are doing fine." JJ just looked at Sandy as if she was telling him about the Easter bunny.

Jack looked at Sandy almost as puzzled as JJ. "You told her he was doing fine?"

"Yes." Sandy replied. "I didn't want to give her bad news over the phone."

"Sandy he has no idea who Brandy is." Jack said.

"I'm sure he will know her when he sees her again." Jack wasn't sure if force feeding JJ memories was going to work. He was torn between wanting his son to get back to normal, and letting the past stay buried.

Jack knew that JJ wanted to know how he came to be in the hospital. Until JJ got better Jack decided to keep it to himself. He left JJ's room and waited to catch Brandy in the hall before she went into the room. He had to tell her not to expect to much from JJ at first.

Jack saw Brandy coming down the hall grinning from ear to ear. He hated that he was going to be the person that killed that happiness.

"Isn't it great Jack?" Brandy said as she through her arm's around Jack's waist and gave him a hug. Jack had his back to Sandy as she came out the door, so he didn't know she was there.

"Brandy there's something I have to tell you go in to see JJ." Jack said as he took Brandy by the arms and backed her up. "JJ has amnesia and he don't know anything about what went on before the accident. You have to be careful of what you say around him."

The smile left Brandy's face as she realized what Jack was saying. "I promised you that I wouldn't tell anyone and I won't, not even JJ."

Sandy was just about to ask what they were talking about but decided to trust Jack. "Isn't it great Mrs. Tall!" Brandy said as she saw Sandy standing there.

"Yes it is. It's great news but from now on you call me Sandy. Besides it's going to be Mrs. Benson soon for real." Jack knew that Sandy's smile and laugh was just to hide the jealousy that was eating her insides. Maybe I got through to her last night. Jack thought.

If there was one thing he would not tolerate was a woman possesed by the green eyed monster. Besides she was jealous of a little girl that was young enough to be his daughter. Some how Jack felt insulted by the whole thing. I wonder what sandy would do if it had been a woman instead of a little girl. Jack followed the girls back into JJ's room. He had to be there when JJ saw Brandy for the first time. If the boy remembered anything she would bring it back to him.

Brandy approached the bed as if she was sneaking up on a baby bird. One wrong move and it would fly away from her. Brandy took her right hand and placed it on JJ's bandaged head before speaking "Baby, do you know who I am?" She asked in a whisper. Tears came to her green eyes as JJ shook his head no.

Jack was as surprised as the others when he saw the tears in JJ's light blue eyes as well. He had to get out of there before he started crying as well. Without saying a word Jack went out the door keeping his back to them all. He had just started down the hall when JJ's doctor yelled for him to wait.

The doctor was standing with a woman with long black hair with her back to him. "Mr. Benson I would like to introduce to you Dr. Christine West." The doctor said. Jack just about passed out when the woman turned around.

The shock on Jack's face was only matched by the look on the doctors face. "Cricket?" Jack asked as he steadied his legs. "Jack is that really you?" Cricket asked.

Both Jack and Cricket through their arms around each other and hugged. A short chubby doctor stared over the rim of his glasses. "I take it you two have met."

"Yes, Doctor Gilman. We are old friends from way back." Cricket said.

"Mr. Benson this is our Neurologist, Doctor Christine West. She will be in charge of JJ Talls case."

"When did you become a Doctor?" Jack asked with excitement.

"About the time you became a con." Cricket said as the smile left both their faces.

"I was just going to see JJ. Would you like to go with me?" Cricket asked.

Jacks mind raced to get himself under control before going back through the door. Sandy's heart dropped when she saw Jack walk through the door with his arm around the waist of a beautiful doctor with long black hair. The only one that didn't find it strange was JJ as he saw the two come in. Maybe Jack is just testing me. Sandy thought before speaking.

"Sandy this is JJ's new doctor." Jack said with his arm still around Cricket's waist.

"Mrs. Tall, I'm Dr. Christine West. I'm a Neurologist and I'm going to do my best to help your son to a full recovery." Cricket said as she held out her hand for Sandy to shake.

"Our son." Sandy said as she took Crickets hand and shook it while looking at Jack. With the look Cricket gave Jack his arm came down to his side in a hurry.

"I'm sorry Mrs. Benson there has been a mix up in the name on your sons chart." Cricket said.

Sandy was about to straighten her out on it but Jack beat her to it. "This is Sandy Tall not Benson yet." Jack added. Cricket stopped trying to figure it out and went to JJ's side.

As soon as Cricket left them standing, Sandy ushered Jack back through the door. again. "Jack Benson, who is that woman in there?" sandy asked pointing to JJ's room as if Jack could be confused as to who she was talking about.

"You heard her, she's JJ's doctor." Jack said then paused before he said anymore.

"I know she's a doctor. What does she have to do with you?"

"I'm starting to think you are letting your jealousy come out." Jack said.

"Is that what this is, some kind of test?" Sandy watched as every muscle in Jack's body tightened.

"She was a girl friend back before we met." Jack told her. Sandy was about to apologize to Jack when he beat her to it. "I'm sorry Sandy. I just wasn't thinking of how you must have felt when we came in."

Sandy reached and cupped Jacks face in her hands. "Do you still have feelings for her?"

"No." Jack said but Sandy wasn't convinced. "Wait till we get home tonight, then I will tell you all about her." Jack was saying as Brandy came out the door and interrupted him.

"The lady doctor said she would be a while so we could go get something to eat." Brandy said as she came out.

A different girl was their waitress. This time she took their order without saying a word. "Was she a doctor when you knew her?" Sandy asked.

"Tonight!" Jack said. "I'll tell you everything tonight." Brandy just sat there and stared blankly at the two of them not daring to ask a question.

"You should have seen JJ smile when that lady told him that her friends call her Cricket." Brandy said as she stopped staring at them.

"Cricket is it?" Sandy asked as she turned her attention to Brandy. "Yes it's her stage name." She said.

"Must have been a stripper with skinny legs." Sandy said not taking her eyes off Jack.

"No, she was a singer in Nashville Tenn." Brandy said without thinking. A smile came to Jacks face before he spoke.

"What else did the lady doctor say to JJ?" Jack asked as if he never knew Cricket.

"She ran me out about that time. So I didn't hear anything else."

"It's to bad that she couldn't tell us her life history in just a few minutes." Jack said smiling at Sandy, who was getting pissed off.

"I sure hope she is good at her job." Brandy said as the waitress brought thier food.

"I'm sure she puts everything she has in whatever job she is doing." Jack said with a big grin. Jack thought that maybe he had gone to far as he looked at Sandy. He could sware that he saw flames in her eyes.

"She had better be good, for my sons sake." Sandy said holding back the words that she wanted to say.

"That's enough about the doctor. Let's enjoy our meal." Jack said as he took his eyes off Sandy.

Cricket decided that it would be best if she didn't look up Jack as she left the hospital. For a long time she had been angry at Jack for just running off when her brother David and Shafaun died. It wasn't until the police let her see the manslaughter charge against Jack that she realized why he ran.

Cricket had never thought of seeing Jack again, let alone put his son life in her hands. JJ is my main concern now, not Jack. Besides that Sandy Tall doesn't act like she would move over that easy. She decided that she would just find herself a new lover, there would be to much trouble with Jack. She had never had a problem finding someone to be her lover. But she had ti admit that as lovers go, Jack was at the top of the list.

After her brothers death, she had went back to collage and got a doctors degree and work had been her bed mate for so long.

Cricket tried to remember the last time she had sex and all she could be sure of was that it was cold and snow was two feet high out side. She and Bill, a man in her class, did it in the parking lot and they damn near froze their asses off. The thought of the time her and Jack had last made love jumped to her mind. "No!" Cricket said out loud. "I'm not going to let myself get hurt by that bastard again."

"I knew that bastard was no good." Kim had told her after Jack had left.

"Talking of bastards that husband of yours was the one who killed my brother and his friend." Cricket had blurted out. As far as she knew they had never caught Tom. All this thinking of the old days was giving Cricket a headache. She looked around the little furnished apartment that she had rented and got more depressed. The next time she got some time off she was going to find a house and get out of this place.

Sandy seemed to calm down after Jack told her the whole story about him and Cricket. Crickets brother David and his girlfriend Shafaun and of course Tom. She had been wrong again by jumping to conclusions. There must be a way she could make it up to him but for now she couldn't think of one. Jack had gone back to his bedroom after they had made love. Sandy had asked him why he slept alone and he told her that he had been alone all his life. He grew to like sleeping alone. Sandy got out of bed and tip toed across the floor.

As she climbed the stairs she almost backed out of going to Jacks room. Jack looked like he was asleep but she could remember the last time she thought that about him. The light coming through the window only shed light on his shoulder and bare chest. His face was laying in the dark so Sandy watched the rise and fall of his chest to see if he was asleep. After she decided that he was she lifted the sheet and lay down beside him.

Jack through his arm over Sandy's bare breast. "Have a bad dream?" Jack asked without moving.

Sandy was glad it was dark so Jack couldn't tell how white she was from the shock his question made her. Without speaking Sandy shook her head yes.

"You going to be alright?" Sandy shook her head again and Jack closed his eyes again. Soon after Sandy closed her eyes, she too was sound asleep. The next morning she awoke with a smile and Jacks erect penis against her butt. She was tempted to put it to good use but decided not to press her luck about sleeping with Jack. She eased her way out of bed and the room before waking Jack. Jack had told her that he hadn't seen Cricket in twenty years so she was sure that the lady doctor wasn't a threat. If you keep screwing up, I'm going to lose him. Sandy said to herself while taking her bath.

Sandy had dressed and fixed them something to eat by the time Jack got up. Jack was just about to take a bite of eggs when Sandy told him that she was going to ask Cricket to come stay with them when JJ came home.

The egg covered fork falling and hitting Jacks plate, echoed down the hall. "I don't think that's a good idea at all." Jack said before swallowing.

"You said that what you two had was in the past, didn't you?" Jack managed to swallow before he answered her.

"Yes but we don't want to invite trouble to live with us the way you are about getting jealouse."

"I'm sure we can act like adults, if you can." Sandy said. "And besides JJ is going to need her long after he gets out of the hospital. Jack had never told Sandy that she couldn't do what she wanted with her house and he wasn't going to start now. He knew that he was in trouble.

JJ sounded like he was talking through his nose but he was talking when Cricket came onto his room. Jack and Sandy hadn't came yet so Cricket tried to find out how much of his past that he could remember.

"Do you know your mother?"

"Ma." JJ said the best he could.

"Ok, do you know your pa?"

"Papa, he's my friend."

"That's right. Your papa is your best friend." Cricket was glad that JJ was making sentences. That meant that his brain was repairing itself.

"Would you like to get out of the bed and go for a ride in a wheel chair?" JJ nodded yes then clapped his hands like a three year old. Cricket had an orderly take JJ to the sun room on the first floor. She went about her work and the room was empty when Jack and Sandy came into the room.

"Jack where is JJ?" Sandy asked in a panic.

"I don't know but you can believe I'm going to find out." Jack said.

Jack and Sandy rushed to the nurses station to ask where JJ had gone. "Dr. West said that he asked to get out so she sent him to the sun room." The RN told them.

"JJ asked to get out?" Jack asked in shock.

"Yes the doctor said he requested to leave." After getting directions to the sun room, the two rushed to the first floor.

"You just keep trying." The black orderly was saying as Jack and Sandy came up to them.

"Papa!" JJ said when he saw them.

"You know you scared the hell out of me." Sandy said as she knelt down beside him. JJ just laughed and clapped his hands. "They said he asked to get out of the room. Is that true?"

"He can put a few words together but I don't know if you would call it talking." The black orderly said.

"Will you talk to pa?" Jack asked JJ.

JJ took Jacks hand and placed it on his cheek. "Papa papa." Was all he would say.

"Will you talk for ma?" Sandy asked as she held out her hand for JJ to take. JJ let go of Jack's hand but he didn't take Sandy's.

"Don't you remember your mother?" JJ shook his head yes but his blank expression never changed. Sandy forced a smile so she wouldn't start crying.

"I'm sorry folks but this young man has got to go back to his room in about ten minutes." The black orderly told them as he headed for the elevator with JJ in front. Jack and Sandy followed in silence.

When the doors of the elevator opened Jack saw Cricket standing, talking to a male doctor that was quit a few years younger.

"I'll be glad to have dinner with you the next time we are both off at the same time." The young man was saying as Jack and Sandy approached.

Sandy was smiling from ear to ear but Jack wore no smile. He remembered how Cricket loved young men, he was living proof.

"Dr. West could we have a word with you in private?" Jack asked as he placed a hand on Crickets shoulder.

"Mr. Benson if you don't mind." Cricket said as she brushed Jack's arm from her shoulders.

It was all Sandy could do to stop herself from bursting out laughing. "I'm sorry I offended you Dr. West, but I do need to talk to you.

"Mr. Benson if you will just go to JJ's room. I'll be in there in a moment when I'm finished." Cricket said. She saw Jacks eyes flash blue fire but she was determined to stand her ground.

Jack walked off without a word not even looking back. Sandy found her body following Jack but her eyes were on Cricket. She had not thought of her as an alie before.

"Did you see that bitch make a fool out of me out there?" Jack asked.

"Jack baby. I love you but you were the one that did that." Sandy said.

"I should have known better then to think I would get any support from you. I'm going to give her a piece of my mind when she gets here." Jack said as he looked toward the door.

A candy stripper came through the door carrying a note from Cricket that simply said come to the Dr. lounge. "I'll be back soon. This won't take long." Jack said as he walked out the door without looking at Sandy.

"How dare you!" Cricket started as soon as Jack came through the door. "I'm a doctor here in this building, not some lover. We knew each other a long long time ago. Do you realize how much trust you just destroyed in the eyes of the other doctors?"

Jack was trying to answer but Cricket wouldn't stop and give him time. "What we had died with my brother and I have no intention of starting it up again."

"I guess I let the green eyed monster bite me." Jack said. "I appologize for acting like we were twenty again."

"You didn't yell at her to bad did you?" Sandy asked as Jack came into the room.

"No, not to bad." Jack said as he went to JJ's side.

"Quick it." JJ said when Cricket came through the door. Both Jack and Sandy's heads turned to JJ with their mouths open.

"Mr. Benson, Jack that young man I was talking to when you interrupted is a brain surgeon and he thinks he can help JJ with an operation."

"What are his chances?" Sandy asked.

"He thinks JJ will have a seventy five percent chance of full recovery and twenty five percent chance of death."

"That's to big a risk." Jack said.

"What is his chance of recovery if he don't have the operation?" Sandy asked.

"Not much better then he is now." Cricket said.

"Do it!" Sandy said. "No!" Jack said. "It's to risky." He rose to a standing position.

"I know my son." Sandy said. "I know he would rather be dead then the way he is now." Jack could see that Sandy had made up her mind.

"I'll need both of your approval. You had better hope that JJ lives cause if he don't, there's going to be hell to pay." Jack reached and grabbed Crickets wrist as she turned to leave.

"Is that young doctor any good?" He asked.

"The best!" Cricket said as she pulled the door open.

"Jack I'm just doing what I think is best."

"For who? You or JJ?" Jack said as he returned to JJ's side.

Sandy found that she couldn't answer Jack's question truthfully. She began doubting her quick decision. Had she put her son's life and Jacks love in jeopardy? Will she walk out of this hospital with nothing but her memories? Sandy was so confused that she just about ran for Cricket and tell her she had changed her mind. The hope that JJ would return to normal was just to high.

"Do you want to be normal again?" Jack asked JJ in a low voice. JJ nodded yes.

It was two days after talking to Cricket that JJ went into the operating room. Jack could only sit down in short periods. The longest time Sandy would guess was ten minutes.

"Jack, JJ is going to be alright. We are in for a long wait so just relax."

"I can't help it Sandy. I feel danger and I don't know why."

"It's just nerves." Sandy said as she patted Jack on the hand.

Six hours later Cricket came into the waiting room to tell them that JJ came through the operation ok. He was still not out of danger yet.

"He's in CCU now and they will move him to his room once he is stablized."

"Oh thank you Crickett!" I'm so greatful for all your help."Sandy said.

"I'm just doing my job but a word of thanks means a lot to me. Cricket said.

"Thank you!" Jack said as he held out his hand.

Sandy and Jack sat for two more hours in JJs room before they brought him in. He had so many tubes coming out of him that that he looked like a sink. Cricket came in to tell them that only one of them could stay in the room at a time.

"I'll stay." Jack said as he didn't wait for Sandy to voleenter before he sat down in the chair.

"You can wait your turn down the hall Mrs. Tall." Cricket said as she walked out the door with Sandy. Jack hadn't been in JJ's room more then thirty minutes, when Sandy came into the room saying there was a detective in the waiting room that wanted to talk to him.

Dale rose from his chair when Jack entered the room. "I hate to bother you old buddy but this can't wait."

"What is it?" Jack asked as the two sat back down.

"Do you know a Tom Hall from back in the sixties?" Dale asked. Just the sound of his name brought chills to Jack.

"Yes, I remember him. He's a bad apple." Jack said.

"We think he killed a girl in Nashville by the name…" Dale paused to look in his notebook. "Kim Harden. The police got to talk to her before she died. She told them that Tom Hall was the one that killed her and he made her tell him where Cricket, I mean Dr. West was living. So we have reason to think he may be coming here. Now what do you think the bad apple wants with the doctor?" Dale was surprised when Jack told him the whole ugly story.

"Have you told Dr. West anything about this?"

"No. Until I had more information I thought it best not to alarm her." Dale said as he rose to leave.

"You just keep an eye on her. I'll tell Cricket what is going on." Jack said as he rose too. "I'll stay by her side. If anyone should know Tom when they see him it's me."

Jack had Dr. West paged and she took him to the doctors lounge again. Jack put his hands on her shoulders. "I've done told you about that Jake." Cricket said in an angry voice.

"Cricket this isn't about sex. It's about your life." Cricket wasn't sure if Jack was playing a joke or not. If it was a joke it was a bad one.

"What do you mean?" She asked in a frightened voice.

"I mean we think we know where Tom Hall will be coming. Here." Jack said pointing a finger at the floor.

"Why would Tom want to come see me? The last time I laid eyes on him was the night before he killed David."

"Maybe you should sit down before I tell you." Jack waited till Cricket was sitting before he went on. "The police in Nashville thinks Tom killed Kim and he made her tell where you were at before he killed her."

"Poor Kim!" Cricket said as she put her hands to her mouth.

"I'm going to take you to your place to pick up your things. You are going to be under house arrest at my house, that is." Jack said.

"Jack I can't do that. I'm a doctor. I can't tell my patients that I can't see them today because some lunitic from my past might see me here."

"Cricket we go back to far for me to take a chance of losing you again. Do you think Tom is trying to bring you flowers?" Jack shouted.

"No! I don't but I'm not going to let him drive me into a hole either." The sound of code blue in 313 came over the loud speaker. Both Jack and Crickets face turned white from shock.

Both of them ran to JJs room as fast as they could go. The RN on duty was already giving JJ electric shock but it was doing no good. Sandy was like a sitting statue in the corner with her unblinking eyes and her mouth open.

"Get her out of here." Cricket said as she took charge of JJ.

"Oh Jack! I'm going to be sick." Sandy said as they came out of the room. Jack walked her to the restrooms and waited out side the door. The look Cricket had on her face told everything without saying a word. She hooked her arm in Jacks and lead him to an empty room. No sooner had they stepped inside, Jack broke down crying.

The sight of him made Cricket start crying as well. When Sandy came out of the restroom, Jack was gone so she asked the RN if she knew where he went. There the nurse said pointing to the room Jack and Cricket was in.

"I'm sorry Jack I did my best but it wasn't good enough." Cricket cried.

"I told her this operation was to dangerous." Jack said as he fought back tears.

"Don't be afraid of crying in front of me Jack. We go back to far is what you told me wasn't it?" Cricket asked as she looked into Jacks blue eyes. Neither Jack or Cricket knew what happened, their lips locked in a kiss.

Jack didn't know that he had his eyes closed until Sandy started screaming 'You bastard' caused him to open them.

"You no good bastard!" Sandy sreamed as she ran down the hall.

"Oh my God!" Jack said as he pushed Cricket aside to run after Sandy. He wasn't even aware that Cricket was right on his heels. Sandy ran out of the hospital and went straight to Jacks car.

She was already sitting in the passenger seat with the door open by the time Jack and Cricket caught up with her. A man stepped out of the shadows in front of Jack holding a gun. Both Jack and Cricket stopped in their tracks.

"Tom!" Cricket said in shock.

"Well I didn't expect to find you here, Jack Benson. This is an added bonus." Tom said as he waved the gun around pointing at Jack and Cricket. "You can thank your friend Kim for telling me where to find you Cricket. She thought I would let her live if she told me. I never understood what I saw in her."

At first Sandy didn't understand why Jack and Cricket just stopped when she saw the man standing with his back to her. She thought he was just asking directions. When she moved to the side she could see that he was holding a gun.

"What am I going to do?" She said as she searched the car over for a weapon. When she opened the glove box she saw that Jack had put his gun in it so he wouldn't be packing a gun in the hospital. As Sandy armed the gun and pulled the trigger the gun wouldn't work.

"Oh my God!" What was she doing wrong? She tried to remember when Jack had showed her how to use her pa's gun so many years ago. Always put the safety on, he had told her. So Sandy turned the gun sideways to find the safety and take it off. With the gun ready to fire Sandy took careful aim at the man and pulled the trigger.

Tom saw the woman with the gun about the time he saw the fire come out of the end of it. Sandy's aim was right on it's mark. The bullet hit Tom in the center of his chest killing him. In Tom's last grip of life, his finger closed around the trigger of his gun and tightened. The gun jerked just enough that the bullet that came out of it hit Cricket in her head.

Jack didn't have to look for life signs, the bullet had gone in the front and out the back taking her brains with it. He turned to see Sandy walking towards him still holding the gun.

"No!" He screamed at the same time he heard two shots go off at the same time. The two bullets picked Sandy up and carried her ten feet back before she hit the ground. Jack threw his arms to his sides in disbelief. As Jack broke from his trance, he heard the officers yell.

"Police! Don't move."

"It's okay boys. This is Jake Benson." Dale told them.

Jack ran to Sandy's side and picked her up in his arms. When Jacks tears fell upon Sandy's face she opened her eyes and smiled at Jack.

"Tell JJ mama loves him." She said before death over took her.

Tears blurred Jacks vision so bad that he took his finger's and closed Sandy's eye's then kissed her for the last time without seeing her. Jack's eye's fell on the gun laying where Sandy had dropped it after being hit. He gently laid Sandy's head down and started for the gun. As Jack stooped to pick it up Dales foot came down on it.

"That's evidence old buddy. You know that." Dale said still holding his gun in his hand.

"Why?!" Jack screamed pointing to the dead.

"All the police chief would give me for this stakeout was two rookies.

They thought she was the one shooting people."

"Dale you said if I ever needed a favor that you would do it." Jack said. "Let me have my gun and walk away."

"I can't do that Jack! Thank God! I can't let you ruin your life either. Place this man under arrest." Dale told the two officers as they came up.

"What are you arresting me for?" Jack shouted as the two handcuffed his hands behind his back.

"I'll think you are drunk or on drugs." Dale said as he led Jack to the police car.

"I'm going to beat your ass so bad when I get out!" Jack said as they put him in the police car.

"Saying you are going to do bodily harm to an officer of the law. See I told you I would think of something." Dale said as he closed the door.

When they got to the jail Dale took Jack to a small room where the officers did exercise. Dale whispered something to the desk clerk before taking Jack to the room and locked the door.

"What's this all about?" Jack asked about the same time Dale pitched a pair of boxing gloves to him.

"If you don't get rid if that hate it will eat you up for the rest of your life. If you need someone to hit on, here I am." Dale said as he put on a pair of gloves too.

"Hitting you won't end my hatred of those two who killed Sandy." Jack said as he tossed the gloves to Dales feet.

"Jack those two men were protecting you or so they thought. They didn't know who was on the other end of that gun. They did the same thing for you as you did for me."

"You stupid bastard, do you think I'm going to feel sorry for those two cowboys, who just killed my life? Now if you'll unlock the door I'll go bury my dead." Jack said as he waited for Dale to let him out.

"If those two are still working tomorrow I'll have your badge." Jack said as he walked out the open door.

"Jack you'll need these." Dale said and when Jack turned Dale tossed him his car keys.

All the way home Jack fought back the need to cry. The house was empty of sound and lights as Jack got out of the car. The house stood as a black shadow against the night sky. Jack remembered the first time he had seen the house and Sandy. Every time Jack pictured Sandy or Cricket in his mind he saw them twenty years ago.

Jack paused before he turned the knob on the unlocked door that let him into the house. The silence was unnerving as the door seemed to open as if Sandy was on the other side of it.

The light didn't make the emptiness of the room go away as he thought it would. It just made Jack aware of just how empty the room was. He had decided that he would just get his things and go to a motel but the feeling that Sandy was there with him changed his mind. There was one place he had to go to before he left again and it had to be early morning when he went.

A rooster crowing outside the window woke Jack up the next morning. Jack hadn't noticed the rooster before but he was there. As Jack opened his eyes he could see that he had been sleeping in Sandy's bed.

He looked for his pants to put on but they wasn't in the room. "I thought I went to bed in my room." Jack said as he headed upstairs to get his pants. He remembered of dreaming of Sandy and her leading him to her room but it was just a dream. He thought in confusion as he saw his pants laying where he put them when he took them off.

Jack put on his pants and started out the door when he noticed Sandy's walking stick sitting by the door. As he picked up the stick Sandy's smiling face flashed in his mind. Instead of driving, Jack walked to the lake. The mist on the water made the water look hot. Jack took off all his clothes and waded into the lake.

Jack waded in until only his head and shoulders were out of the water. Sandy's voice came out of the mist saying "close your eyes." His blue eyes scanned the lake to see where the sound had come from but he didn't see anything.

At first Jack started to get out of the water because this was strange even for him.

"Please" He heard the voice say.

"What have I got to lose?" Jack said and closed his eyes. He could hear ripples in the water as if someone was approaching. As he tried to open his eyes he could feel Sandy's small fingers holding them closed.

Jack reached out in front of him and his palms felt like they were on Sandy's breast. Afraid to open his eyes for fear of losing the feel of Sandy, he left his eyes closed.

"My dear love, you must go on alone from here so just remember I will always be with you. I love you!" The voice said before it faded away.

"Don't go!" Jack was saying as he opened his eyes. Only the warm mist of the lake could hear his request.